Growing Azaleas

Allan Evans

Kangaroo Press

Acknowledgments

The author wishes to thank the following people for their assistance:

Sue and Tony Doyle, Mt Tootie Nursery, for providing plants for photography,
Judy Horton for providing her notes and photographs,
Lee Evans for providing the line drawings and typing the manuscript,
Bob Cherry for advice on plant breeding,
Ben Swane, Swane's Nursery, for information on Plant Variety Rights,
John Slykerman, Kenny Lane Nursery, for advice on new varieties,
Trevor Edwards for providing plants for photography,
Kellie Rees for typing the manuscript,
and the staff of Mt Tootie Nursery for general assistance.

Line drawings by Lee and Allan Evans
Photographs by Jaime Plaza, Judy Horton and Peter Bundock

Cover: 'Madame Auguste Haerens'

© Allan Evans 1994

First published in 1994 by Kangaroo Press Ltd
3 Whitehall Road Kenthurst NSW 2156 Australia
P.O. Box 6125 Dural Delivery Centre NSW 2158 Australia
Printed in Hong Kong by Colorcraft Ltd

ISBN 0 86417 083 1

Contents

1 The Classification and History of Azaleas

Botanists keep telling us that azaleas are part of the genus *Rhododendron*. While gardeners are quite happy to admit the botanists may be right they still call an azalea an azalea—and know exactly what they are talking about! Azaleas make up a distinct group of plants that are loved in many parts of the world. The name 'azalea' comes from the Greek word for dry or parched and probably refers to the plants' ability to grow in warm climates.

Originally it was thought that all azaleas were deciduous and all rhododendrons evergreen, but the discovery of evergreen azaleas saw the end of that distinction. Now they are classed as being part of the azalea series in the *Rhododendron* genus.

There are more than 800 species of rhododendrons and, of these, approximately 40 species are evergreen azaleas. In many cases the species have become so intermingled that the differences are now quite blurred, although there are several well-recognised subdivisions. The main evergreen groups within the azalea series could be classed as Belgian-Indian, Tall Single Indica, Kurume, Satsuki and Gumpo, while the common deciduous groupings are Mollis, Ghent, Exbury, and Knap Hill hybrids.

In spite of the fact that they are now grown in many parts of the world, azaleas come from a fairly limited area. Evergreen azaleas are native to Asia, while deciduous azaleas come from parts of Asia, southern Europe and North America. Many have been crossed to produce hybrids that display some of the characteristics of both parents. In most cases, evergreen azaleas are only crossed with other evergreen azaleas and deciduous azaleas hybridised with other deciduous azaleas.

Azaleas have been cultivated in Japan for more than 400 years, which makes it difficult to work out which were the original varieties. Because Japan kept itself locked off from the rest of the world for so long, azaleas became part of the Japanese 'mystique', and were highly desired by westerners who caught occasional glimpses of them in Chinese gardens. It was only when Japan was opened to foreigners in the nineteenth century that the wealth of azaleas became available to eager plant collectors. This occurred at the same time as some of the great European gardens were being established, where it was found that the deciduous varieties flourished outdoors. The more cold-sensitive evergreen azaleas could only be grown in conservatories built to house tender plants.

As azaleas became more readily available in Europe they were hybridised to produce new varieties. In the early part of the nineteenth century, a Belgian baker in the town of Ghent began crossing the hardy, scented *Rhododendron luteum* with some of the American species. Through these crosses he produced the first of a famous strain that is still known as the Ghent hybrids.

The original Ghent hybrids were deciduous but other growers in the town worked with evergreen plants from Asia to develop the well-known Belgian-Indian azaleas. Despite the name, the Belgian-Indian plants did not come from India. The plants were bred from *Rhododendron simsii*, a Chinese species that is sometimes classified as *Rhododendron indicum*. The name 'indicum' was given because of the western tendency to class anything from the east as being Indian.

The Belgian-Indian hybrids were not cold hardy in Europe and were grown as flowering indoor plants. Some were taken to the United States as flowering houseplants where it was found that they were able to grow outdoors in the southern states. This gave rise to a new breed of Indica azaleas which were named Southern Indicas.

Other evergreen azaleas have been developed in Japan. Perhaps the most characteristically Japanese are the Kurume azaleas derived from the species *Rhododendron kiusianum*. Kurumes have a denser and more twiggy growth than the Indica azaleas. The dense growth responds well to clipping; a characteristic which appeals to the Japanese preference for neat and controlled gardens. They are often used in the west to give a Japanese 'feel' to a garden.

Kurumes were introduced to California by a Japanese horticulturist, Kojiro Akoshi, from the city of Kurume. In 1917 the British plant collector E.H. Wilson, who at the time was working for the Arnold Arboretum in the United States, visited Japan and selected fifty of Akoshi's best plants to take back to America. These plants became known as Wilson's Fifty and did much to popularise the use of Kurume azaleas. It was found that they could be grown in a wider climatic range than other evergreen azaleas because they were much hardier, both to cold conditions and dryness.

Gumpo azaleas, a collection of small-growing evergreen varieties, were also developed in Japan and Formosa (Taiwan). These compact bun-shaped plants are derived from the species *Rhododendron eriocarpum*. Their use is confined to temperate mountain areas as they flower late in spring and the flowers can be spoiled by warm spring weather. Their dense foliage is thought to make them more susceptible to fungal diseases such as petal blight.

Two famous lines of azaleas were developed in England at Knap Hill and Exbury. Anthony Waterer of Knap Hill Nursery began working with deciduous azaleas in the 1860s and hybridised a wide range of beautiful plants. He concentrated on producing cultivars that were hardy enough to grow outdoors in the English climate. In the twentieth century many of the Knap Hill hybrids were further developed by Lionel de Rothschild of Exbury. He was particularly attracted to one plant with huge yellow blooms, which he used to pollinate most of the other azaleas in his collection. From these crosses he developed a wonderful range of plants with characteristic round heads of flowers. His garden became a showcase for deciduous azaleas and even now many of the Exbury hybrids are still readily available.

The Mollis hybrids were developed in Holland in the early 1840s from a cross between *Rhododendron molle* from China and *Rhododendron japonicum* from Japan. The result was a line of deciduous hybrids in a range of brilliant colours including yellow, orange, apricot, peach and various shades of red. Whites and creams are also available. The Mollis azaleas are tall, upright growing plants to 2 m high and almost as wide. In cooler areas they can be grown in slight shade or full sun.

Although some of the Mollis, Knap Hill and

Exbury azaleas are grown in Australia, their appeal is limited because, like the Gumpos, they flower late in spring and are often affected by spells of hot weather. This confines their use to areas of high altitude with cool spring temperatures. The mild Australian winters and warm summers are generally far more suited to the growing of evergreen azaleas.

Azalea Flower Forms

Azalea flowers vary widely in appearance. The main differences are in the form, colour and size of the blooms. Single blooms are the most common flower type. The diagram below shows the elements that comprise a typical single flower.

The corolla is made up of five petals which join at the base to form a wide-mouthed trumpet. The standard or dorsal petal is flanked by two pairs of petals known as the upper and lower wings.

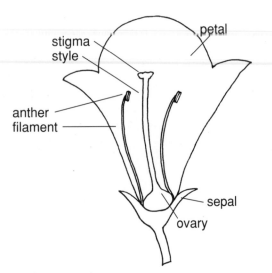

Azalea flower structure

The calyx at the base of the corolla consists of five individual sepals. The sepals are green and only a few millimetres in length. The stalk is small and joins the base of the calyx.

The pistil or female component of the flower is made up of the ovary at the base, the style arising from the ovary and the sticky pollen-collecting stigma at the top of the style.

The stamens which form the male organ of the flower originate at the base of the corolla and consist of the filament and the anther which carries the pollen.

Azalea breeders have developed five variations of the single bloom.

In semi-double varieties the stamens form additional modified petals, which are often distorted or contorted, arranged in the centre of the flower.

In double-flowered varieties the stamens have been developed to the point where they closely resemble another set of petals in the centre of the bloom.

Hose-in-hose describes blooms in which the sepals form a complete new trumpet. Two trumpet-like sets of blooms form one inside the other, but are offset so that the petals alternate. The semi-double and double characteristics have also been developed in conjunction with the hose-in-hose formation, so that we now have semi-double hose-in-hose and double hose-in-hose flowers.

It is not unusual to see different types of flowers occurring on the one plant. For example, petaloids may develop in the centre of a single bloom, in effect creating a semi-double flower.

Blooms occurring outside the normal flowering period sometimes display unusual characteristics. Such variations in colour or form are not stable and later blooms will be true to type. This phenomenon is not to be confused with sporting which is a genetic mutation. Sporting may show as variations in flowers, leaves or growth habit. When the

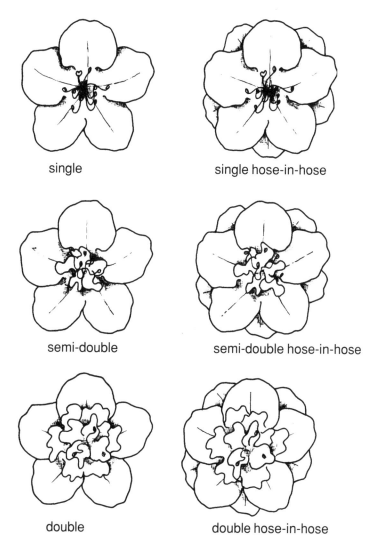

single

single hose-in-hose

semi-double

semi-double hose-in-hose

double

double hose-in-hose

Azalea flower forms

portion of plant is isolated and used for propagation, it will continue to exhibit the new characteristic.

Plant breeders are continually alert to the possibilities of developing new variations in flowers by the use of sporting. Some varieties sport quite freely. 'Paul Schame' is a notable example. However, not all sports are commercially beneficial. A few years ago a sport appeared in 'Searchlight', a slow growing but free flowering azalea. The sport gave vigorous rapid growth, but unfortunately did not produce flowers and had to be discarded.

2 Selecting and Planting Azaleas

There is a vast difference in the quality of azalea plants offered for sale in garden centres. Quite often even the nursery staff do not recognise this difference. It is important to know how to recognise the desirable features of an azalea and make your selection on a sound basis.

Firstly, the leaves will give a clear indication of the health of the plant and although the degree of foliage glossiness varies between varieties, a healthy plant will have a sheen on the foliage. You should avoid buying plants with dull, lifeless-looking leaves.

Don't be distracted by the flowers on the plant. Even if the plant is in full bloom in the nursery, by the time you arrive home the flowers will probably form a carpet in the boot of your car. Look beyond the bloom and examine the frame of the shrub. You should avoid tall, sparse, 'woody' plants. A vigorous, prospering plant will be compact and many branched with an abundance of green shoots and new growth. These are features lacking in a 'woody' specimen. Test that the plant is firm in the pot and does not wobble.

Buy plants that are as advanced as your budget will allow, up to 250 mm pot size. If your budget is tight and you have to buy plants in smaller pots, say 125 mm, the plants will find it difficult to compete with weeds and even other azaleas planted alongside.

You can ensure smaller azaleas get off to a sound start by planting them into a larger-sized pot filled with a recommended azalea potting mix. To grow the newly potted plants to their full potential you will need to give them the same kind of attention that a commercial grower would provide. This means:

1. When potting press the plant firmly into the mix but don't plant it deeper than the original soil level.

2. Leave soil about 25 mm below the rim of the pot to allow for watering.

3. After potting fill the pot with water and allow to drain away, then repeat. This settles the soil around the plant, filling any cavities.

4. Apply a long-term pelleted fertiliser such as Nutricote or Osmocote to the surface of the pot. A dessertspoon of fertiliser is sufficient for a 200 mm pot. I prefer using a mixture of $^1/_3$ three to four month and $^2/_3$ eight to nine month fertiliser, but eight to nine month fertiliser alone is quite satisfactory.

5. Remove flower buds from the plant so that its energy goes into growth not flowering.

6. Place pots in an area where they are protected from direct sunlight, although morning sun (up to 10.30 a.m. in summer) is not likely to cause any problems.

7. If plants need shaping, prune at this stage in accordance with the notes on pruning.

Having carried out these steps, maintenance is the next priority. Because azalea mixes are porous to ensure good drainage, the pots will need regular watering. This means filling the pot with water about every second day in warmer weather, with allowances made for rain. Rain can cause problems in a program like this, as a light shower is not likely to provide as much moisture as regular watering, and despite light rain the plants can become dry and droop visibly. In the cooler months watering can be reduced to twice a week.

Tip pruning of new growth will ensure the plants remain shapely and well branched. This should be carried out when the new growth reaches approximately 75 mm in length. Liquid fertilising through the warmer months is also desirable.

In twelve months' time the plants should be large enough to cope with a reasonable level of competition and can be planted in their permanent position in the garden.

An alternative to the method outlined above is to prepare a nursery area in a well-drained semi-shaded situation and plant the small azaleas directly into the bed. The space between plants could be as little as 300 mm. Less frequent watering will be needed although attention will have to be given to weeding of the bed to reduce competition. Azaleas do not mind being transplanted so it will be a simple task to relocate the azaleas to their final positions in the garden.

If you have planned an azalea planting and decided which varieties you require, then I suggest you take your shopping list to a garden centre in which you have confidence. Ask them to order your chosen varieties from the grower. This should be done in July because the plants prepared for spring sales will have reached their full potential even though few sales would have been made at this stage. This means the grower will still have most of his crop from which to select your chosen varieties. He will base his selection on size, shape and quality as the plants will not be in bloom at this time of year. You will be able to plant them into their desired places before they commence blooming in late August and into September in most areas.

Planting procedures

Careful handling during planting will ensure the plant's subsequent blooming is not unduly affected. When planting directly into the garden bed, first dig over the area, incorporating well-rotted compost and animal manure to a spade's depth. Dig a hole at least $1\frac{1}{2}$ times the size of the pot in which the plant is growing.

Take the plant carefully from the pot. This is easily done by placing the fingers and thumb of one hand on each side of the stem at the soil level and turning the pot upside down. A firm pat on the bottom of the pot with the other hand should loosen the plant and the pot can then be lifted off, leaving the plant and root ball sitting in the palm of the hand. If a firm pat does not free the plant then it is likely that the plant is too dry and requires a good watering before the procedure is repeated.

Place the plant in the hole. The depth at which it was planted in the pot must be maintained. If the hole is too deep, fill with top soil until the level is correct. When the correct depth is attained, place the plant and half fill the hole with top soil. Press the soil until firm, then fill to the top of the hole and firm again.

Form a saucer-shaped depression for collection of water and then give plant a good watering to settle the soil.

If you feel some of your plants are not compatible in terms of colour, vigour or size, remember that they can be lifted and replaced without suffering a setback. In this respect they are extremely flexible components of your garden.

3 Caring for Azaleas

Azaleas are hardy, long-lived plants, and once established, they require very little maintenance. Ample evidence of their longevity can be seen in many established formal gardens in Australia. Much of the spring splendour in these gardens is provided by azaleas as old as fifty years. There are, however, certain conditions that must be met in establishing and maintaining a successful planting.

Azaleas require an acid soil. In terms of pH readings this means 4.5 to 5.5, however I have been surprised to find azaleas growing very vigorously in potting mixes where the pH reading was 6.2. At this level it is important to keep a very close watch for evidence of iron deficiency, which is characterised by yellowing of the leaves with prominent dark green veining.

From a gardener's point of vew, the easiest way to obtain a pH reading of the soil is by using a simple test kit developed by the CSIRO. The kit is available at garden centres.

The testing procedure is simple: a representative sample of soil is taken from the site and moistened with the liquid supplied in the kit. A white powder is sprinkled over the moistened sample. As the powder changes colour a reading is obtained by comparing it with the colour chart provided in the kit.

While the general pH level in your garden may be within the recognised limits for azaleas, there could be localised areas which are unsuitable. Recent construction work involving the use of cement, such as walls, brick fences, new house additions, paths, etc., may affect adjacent garden beds, rendering them unsuitable for azaleas. In this case the soil will need to be acidified before planting azaleas. Iron sulphate sprinkled over the area and watered in is the simplest method. As much as 750 grams per square metre is needed where the pH reading is 7.0; this can be reduced to 350 grams where the reading is 6.0. Acidifying can also be achieved by incorporating flowers of sulphur or tan bark into the soil, but this will require close monitoring because the resulting change of pH occurs over a longer period.

Azaleas do not appreciate waterlogged soil, particularly in winter. Drainage is therefore a prime consideration when selecting a suitable site. If the soil is heavy clay, forget about azaleas unless you are prepared to go to some trouble to improve the drainage. Clay soils can be opened up by working in rotted horse manure and/or gypsum. Agricultural drainage pipes can also be laid to alleviate the problem and the garden can be built up using a recommended azalea growing medium. If you have doubts as to the advisability of growing azaleas in your garden seek advice from a local garden centre.

Watering azaleas can be a problem for new gardeners until they understand the plants' requirements. The azalea's root system is very shallow and dense so it is important to soak the ground around the plant. When planting, form a saucer-shaped depression around the plant as this will help the soil to retain water. In time, with normal garden activities the depression may become filled in or damaged and it is then that the risk of drying out arises, particularly on sloping sites. If you need to restore the depression, do not dig around the plant as this will disturb the roots. Instead bring a bucketful or two of soil to the plant and form it into the required shape.

When the shrub is in full bloom its water requirements are far heavier than in the middle of winter. A soaking twice weekly should suffice. However, in extremely hot weather or if the plant droops and is obviously dried out it will need more. If the water remains in a puddle under the plant for say more than fifteen minutes after watering is completed, then drainage could be a problem.

A mulch, such as cow manure or well-rotted compost, can be placed under the plants to help retain moisture in the soil. Keep in mind that the depth should be no more than about 3 cm to avoid smothering the plants.

The Sun and Azaleas

In recent years there has been a move to promote azaleas as suitable plants for growing in full sun. Most azaleas will grow quite happily exposed to full sunlight; however their blooms will burn and deteriorate quite rapidly in such a position. The ideal situation, even for those varieties designated as 'full sun', is one where they are protected from hot westerly winds and afternoon sun. Azaleas in full sun will need extra watering and mulching as flowering approaches.

Anyway why is it necessary to plant azaleas in full sun? It seems pointless to nurture a bed of plants for ten months in the expectation of a glorious spring display lasting for two months only to have the whole plan wrecked by one extraordinarily hot day. The alternatives to azaleas are seemingly endless. So many of our native shrubs and exotic annuals and perennials thrive in just such a location.

Azaleas in an exposed position protected by a lattice trellis supporting a deciduous climber.

If you have a fully exposed position where you simply must have a bed of azaleas then give thought to erecting a simple covering trellis of lattice or the like. A deciduous climber such as a wisteria, ornamental grape, or perhaps a climbing rose, would protect the azalea blooms when they need it most.

If planting in the open the number of varieties suitable becomes quite limited—tall singles mostly, and just a few doubles which are generally reds or whites. Pink, mauve and most white varieties burn around the petal margins and become unsightly when exposed to hot sun, while even those varieties recommended as suitable will burn if the petals are wet when hit by direct strong sunlight.

Sun tolerant varieties
Singles: 'Alphonse Anderson', 'Alba Magna', 'Jean Alexandra', 'Exquisite', 'Magnifica', 'Rose Magnifica', 'Phoenicea', 'White Lace', 'Pink Lace', 'Duc de Rohan', 'Fielder's White', 'Festival Queen'.

Doubles: 'Redwing', 'Lucille 'K', 'White Bouquet', 'Goyet', 'Mission Bells', 'Red Poppy', 'Waka Kayede', 'Jennifer Ann'.

Nutrition

In their native environment the forerunners of our cultivated azaleas struggled to exist in poor soils leached of calcium, magnesium and potassium. The soils were low on the pH scale, yet remained high in iron and aluminium. Over the passage of time the plants adapted and thrived under these conditions

They are not, therefore, voracious feeders and plants can be damaged readily by too liberal doses of fertiliser. On the other hand, plants which are not provided with sufficient nutrients will have an unthrifty appearance. The answer is of course balance in fertilising.

Well-rotted animal manure, particularly cow manure, used as a loose mulch under plants breaks down to provide nutrients and humus to the soil and at the same time acts to retain moisture. Where the soil is clay based and heavier, horse manure is an aid to opening up the soil. It is not recommended that poultry manure be applied to azaleas repeatedly. While one application may produce obvious beneficial results, regular doses each year can cause an unhealthy rise in the pH level.

The essential elements—nitrogen, phosphorus and potassium—can be provided through the use of artificial fertilisers purchased from a nursery or garden centre. When buying, stipulate that you need an azalea fertiliser and apply it carefully to the top of the soil under the plant but away from the base. If a fertiliser is used that does not convey a recommendation for azaleas, apply it at no more than half the rate stipulated for general nursery use.

A range of long-term slow release pelleted fertilisers is now available. These are prepared with varying ratios of the essential elements and again the advice of the garden centre operator will be invaluable when selecting an appropriate one for azaleas. They are usually marketed in either a three to four month or an eight to nine month formulation. The eight to nine month form is most suitable for azaleas and can be applied on the soil surface after flowering in the spring. If a mulch is provided at the same time, the plants' yearly fertilising requirements will have been met. Nutricote is recommended for its safety as some brands have been known to release salts too freely in hot weather, resulting in severe damage to plants.

Fertiliser burn can be recognised by the browning and shrivelling of growing tips. It starts at the tip, extending fairly rapidly back over the length of the leaf. When this occurs remove the fertiliser manually and water copiously to leach the chemical out of the soil. If this problem arises in plants in tubs or pots, obtain a reliable potting mix and repot as soon as possible.

When the plants are growing freely through the summer months a monthly watering with a liquid fertiliser is beneficial. Several brands are available, some of which are based on seaweed and fish oil extracts. All are safe when used carefully. Again, if no specific rate for azaleas appears on the label, then use at half the rate recommended for general garden use.

Never use liquid fertilisers on plants that are in need of water as damage will result. Meet the moisture needs of the plant first and apply liquid fertiliser as a second operation.

Pruning

Pruning is a vital procedure in the early stages of an azalea's growth. The flower buds form at the terminal ends of stems so the more stems there are on the plant, the more flowers will form!

As a flower comes to the end of its blooming period, two shoots appear at the base of the bloom. These continue the growth cycle and set bud for the next flowering season. As the plant advances in maturity the new growth from below spent blooms becomes shorter and the flowers form closer to one another. Mature plants, therefore, only require maintenance pruning such as the removal of dead wood

Azalea plant before pruning.

Azalea plant immediately after pruning.

'Redwing' pruned to maintain the typical spreading habit of the variety.

and restoration of shape if the growth is becoming unruly.

It is in the early years of growth that careful pruning is necessary. Left to its own devices a rooted cutting will generally have one main leader that continues to grow upwards without much lateral growth. The leader should be arrested before it reaches 150 mm in height. By pruning so that about three pairs of leaves remain, growth will be forced from the junction of each leaf with the stem. When these shoots reach about 70 to 80 mm in length the growing tips should be pinched out between the thumb and forefinger.

Pruning should be carried out when the new growth commences after blooming, through the summer until mid-April. As azaleas need about 20 weeks to set buds on new growth, pruning beyond this stage will interfere with spring blooming.

In conjunction with this pruning program the plants should be kept growing vigorously by the use of fertilisers. You cannot expect optimum results from struggling plants.

Pruning deciduous azaleas
Deciduous azaleas remain leafless until spring then commence flowering and sprouting new leaves simultaneously. Like the evergreen azaleas, the flower buds are carried at the end of the stems, although the plants do not require the same attention to pruning in the early years of growth. Pruning is only carried out to remove unruly growth. This includes cutting back vigorous new growth initiating from the base of the plant to ensure branching and general bushiness. Maintenance pruning is normally carried out in late summer.

4 Landscaping with Evergreen Azaleas

Azaleas prefer a semi-shaded situation so their most effective use in the landscape will be where tall trees cast shade or on the southern side of buildings. Because most shrubs prefer sunny sites, azaleas have a special niche in the well-planned garden.

Indica azaleas

Single Southern Indicas are hardy and have a tall upright growth habit. In good conditions they reach three metres in height while still remaining dense. The spring flower display begins around the middle of September and lasts up to three weeks.

Amongst this group it would be difficult to bypass 'Alba Magna' for a spectacular white display. 'Alphonse Anderson' (dark pink), 'Jean Alexandra' (light pink), 'Phoenicia' (violet)and 'Splendens' (magnificent salmon-pink) are also very attractive inclusions in landscape plantings.

The double and semi-double Indicas are available in a wide range of flower sizes, shapes and colours. Flower colours range from white through to pinks of all shades, reds, mauves and purple, and include many variegated shades. They also vary in degrees of hardiness, height and competitiveness. In this latter category careful selection of varieties is particularly important. Some are more suited to growing in tubs on a sheltered patio for the first five years before planting into the garden.

There is also a wide variation in length of flowering: some varieties carry at least an odd bloom in all but the hottest couple of months of the year, others are restricted to the spring flush.

'Balsaminaeflora', a double Indica, is a particularly worthy inclusion in landscape plantings. It has an attractive groundcover-like habit and salmon-coloured flowers. As well as giving a late spring bloom it flowers again in February. The bloom has many petals (about 40) like a formal camellia and the buds have a rosebud likeness.

Kurume azaleas

Kurume azaleas are sometimes referred to as 'miniatures' or 'dwarfs'. This terminology is quite misleading. Although the flowers and leaves are small, some varieties can reach a similar height to the single Indicas. However, like the Indicas, there is a great variation in height and spread and before planting a particular Kurume into a site its growth potential must be examined.

Because of the small size of the individual blooms, 'spot' blooms will go largely unnoticed. The spring flowering, however, is explosive. Silvery-pink 'Kirin' is a universal favourite. 'Ward's Ruby' (a magnificent red), 'Fairy Queen' (pink), 'Snowflake' (white) and the newcomer 'Fairy Bells' (pink flecks) are all worthy of consideration for planting in the garden.

Kurumes are also highly suitable as hedge

plantings because their dense growth and compact shape responds well to pruning. Some of the hedges created from Kurumes have been in existence for many years in Japan. The Indica varieties are less suited to hedge plantings because their more open growth habit makes them susceptible to damage from animals forcing their way through the barrier.

Pink-flowering 'Kirin' clipped to form a hedge.

Satusuki and Gumpo azaleas

Satsukis, and the closely related Gumpo azaleas, should also be considered in landscape plantings. However, in temperate areas the length of the flowering period of Satsukis can be unreliable as the blooming coincides with the onset of hot weather in November.

The Satsukis have very large single blooms. These may occur with several variations in colour on the one plant, as bicolours in segments or splashes, or self blooms of one or the other of two shades.

Gumpos are particularly useful in landscaping because of their low spreading habit. They look especially attractive planted in a rockery or a pot. The plants reach a height of only half a metre but may be as broad as $1^1/_2$ metres. The flowers are white and in shades of pink. Variegated forms are also available. The single blooms are spectacular but again heed the warning that they may not be showy for long during hot weather.

Azaleas in mass plantings

With the range available, it is not hard to imagine a solid bank of azaleas against a fence or wall, made up of tall-growing single Indicas as the backdrop. Against these, Kurumes could be pruned to maintain a height comfortably below that of the singles. The third row, and maintaining the declining height, would consist of doubles of the long-flowering types, while in front Gumpos and low-growing Indicas such as 'Balsaminaeflora' would be planted to complete the slope to ground level.

The use of white-flowering azaleas in the landscape should not be overlooked. A generous sprinkling of white blooms in mixed plantings brings into focus and highlights the other colours with spectacular results. Some of the most effective plantings of large singles I have viewed have been created against a background of the large white 'Alba Magna' variety.

Other Uses for Evergreen Azaleas

Potted azaleas

Some of the less robust azaleas should be planted in a container, at least until they reach a diameter of 50 cm. In this form they can be positioned on a patio, porch, verandah, or the like. Depending on the weight of the container and the strength of the grower they may be taken indoors when in full bloom for decorative use. If the latter course is adopted, the time the plant spends indoors should be limited to about three weeks at a stretch. If central heating is in use, then perhaps two weeks should be the limit of the plant's stay inside.

Of course the potted azalea will need watering during this period and some sort of impervious container will be necessary to trap the water draining through the pot.

When deciding on the type of container to be used, keep the following thoughts in mind. If you intend to use the plants indoors, plastic pots are light weight and easy to move. Beyond the 250 mm size, even plastic pots become unwieldy. If something larger is sought for outdoors, wooden half casks or concrete tubs are suitable. New concrete tubs will need to be seasoned before use to prevent excessive levels of lime leaching from the pot into the soil. This is achieved by scrubbing both the inside and outside with vinegar which neutralises the alkalinity of the concrete. Concrete pots which have been used previously for growing plants will be quite safe.

Potting into containers is described in the chapter 'Selecting and Planting Azaleas', but again I stress the importance of obtaining a reliable azalea mix as the planting medium. Place the potted azaleas in a semi-shaded position; afternoon sun-drenched situations are out of the question. Remember to water regularly. Drooping leaves and flowers are indications of dryness, however waterlogged pots are a bigger threat to the health of azaleas than the occasional lack of water.

Azaleas as alternatives to cut flowers

Flowering azaleas are an excellent alternative to cut flowers. With the prices of cut flowers at their present levels, it is practical and indeed economical to purchase blooming azaleas in containers from 125 mm up to 200 mm. They can be kept indoors for the period of their flowering and then planted in the garden or even discarded if no suitable position is available when the blooms are spent. Whilst indoors the container could be placed on a pot plant stand made of timber or similar material with a built-in drainage saucer. After the azalea finishes flowering an indoor plant could be placed on the stand.

Azaleas in hanging baskets

Surprisingly, some azaleas make excellent specimens in hanging baskets. It is essential to choose a variety that will 'flow' out of the pot and in the initial growing period the plant must be pruned to reduce upright growth and encourage long lateral leaders.

The following varieties are particularly suited to growing in hanging baskets:

'Comtesse de Kerchove', 'Southern Aurora', 'Silver Anniversary', 'Mission Bells', 'Redwing', 'Rose Queen', 'Rose King', 'Snow Prince', 'White Prince', 'Blushing Princess', 'Dancer', 'Sweet Nellie', 'Violacea' and 'Only One Earth'.

Suitable Kurumes include 'Kirin', 'Christmas Cheer', 'Asa Gasumi', 'Kasane Kagaribi' and 'Violetta'.

Hanging baskets should be watered even more regularly than other container-grown azaleas as they tend to dry out rapidly. If the position allows, remove the attached drainage saucer so that the water drains through the pot unimpeded. After two to three years the plant should be removed from the hanging basket and placed either in the garden or in a large container.

Standard azaleas

Where a specimen plant is desired, standard azaleas may be the answer. These are usually tall-growing single varieties, such as 'Alba

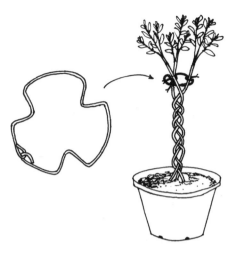

Plait of three standard azaleas. Heads are separated to prevent overcrowding of leaves and stems using a circle of wire with notches bent into it.

Magna', 'Alphonse Anderson' or 'Jean Alexandra', which have been trained to grow as a single stem to a height of approximately one metre before branching is allowed and encouraged. Upright shoots are pruned out to create a spreading, pendulous effect. In full bloom the plants are quite spectacular.

Periodically it is necessary to strip emerging shoots from the stem to maintain the form of the standard. A stake is also needed to support the stem.

In strong winds, there is a tendency for standards grown in light plastic pots to tip over. One way of overcoming this problem is to plait three standard-grown azaleas together while they are in the formative stages. This gives a more robust standard and allows for the use of a less obvious stake. Three plants are selected—these may be of different varieties if desired—and placed together in a large container. The stems are then plaited, preferably on a warm day when they are more pliable, as tightly as the stems will allow. A circle of tie wire with notches bent into it may be placed at the top of the plaited stems and

each stem is then tied into a notch, keeping the three heads separate.

In about two years the stems will weld together so that they become almost indistinguishable. The stems should be stripped regularly to maintain the standard shape. If three different coloured varieties have been used, a barber's pole effect can be achieved by allowing the plants to shoot from the stems and then using judicious pruning to maintain a columnar shape.

Plaited standard azalea stems. Left: Two months after plaiting. Right: Six months after plaiting.

Bonsai
For many years azaleas have been used in bonsai work. Suitable varieties include 'Christmas Cheer', 'Kasane Kagaribi', 'Kirin', 'Ward's Ruby', and indeed any of the small-leaved Kurume varieties. The Satsukis have also been used very effectively by Japanese bonsai growers, although my own preference is for bonsais to carry smaller blooms.

As bonsai culture is well covered in many specialist publications and as I cannot claim any expertise in this area, I suggest that you contact a local bonsai expert for further information.

5 Propagation

Propagation of evergreen azaleas from cuttings is a simple process, although before taking cuttings you should ask yourself: 'Why am I doing this?' If you answer: 'To save money', then I suggest you forget about it. It will take two years for a well-grown cutting to reach the size sold in garden centres for a couple of dollars. Moreover, when you purchase a plant you have the opportunity to select a new variety, whereas your cutting will be a clone of the parent plant. If, however, your answer is: 'Because I love plants and derive pleasure from working with them', then I would say: 'Go right ahead and the very best of luck!'

Cutting propagation takes place when the new season's growth following blooming is firm but not hard or brittle. In most areas cuttings can be taken in December, providing you work in the morning on a mild day.

Select new growth about 75–100 mm in length and cut with sharp secateurs. Strip the leaves away, allowing the growing tip with its surrounding leaves to remain. Rooting compound, which is a growth hormone, can be applied to the lower 25 mm of the prepared cutting. However, this is not essential.

The propagation medium is prepared using one part peat moss to three parts of coarse river sand. Wash the sand so that silt is removed. Break up the peat until it is fluffy but be careful not to overdo this procedure as the peat can be leached out if it is pulverised. The peat will help the medium to retain sufficient moisture while still allowing the mix to drain freely. Mix the two ingredients loosely.

Fill small pots with the mix and firm it in, leaving about 20 mm between the top of the pot and the level of the mix. Water well to settle the medium and remove air pockets, then push the prepared cuttings into the medium to a depth of approximately 25 mm.

Make a 'U'-shaped loop from tie-wire and push it into the pot as shown in the diagram overleaf. Cover with a plastic bag and tie the neck of the bag securely around the pot. Watering can be carried out by standing the pot in a tray of water for about five minutes at a time, then removing and allowing to drain.

Keep the pot in a semi-shaded position (although morning sun will not cause problems) until the cutting has struck. Root hairs should begin to develop in about six weeks and new shoots should appear within a few more weeks. At three months the small

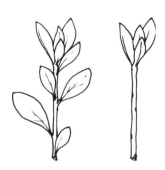

Cuttings before and after preparation.

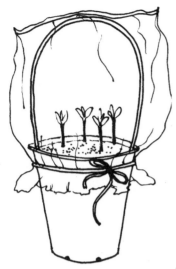

Making a mini glasshouse for cuttings using a loop of wire covered by a plastic bag.

Tray filled with cuttings.

watering may also be a problem: many cuttings are lost through neglecting to water regularly. This occurs especially because of the time taken for the cuttings to reach plant proportions.

Layering

Layering is a convenient method of propagating evergreen azaleas using the following procedure:

From a mature plant select a low-growing branch and bring it unbroken down to ground level. Make a cut in the underside of the branch sloping toward the growing tip of the branch at an angle of about 45 degrees. The cut should extend halfway through the branch. Insert a toothpick or something similar crosswise in the cut to keep it open. Make a staple shaped like a 'U' from wire of a suitable thickness. Place the staple over the branch on the parent plant side of the cut and push it into the ground so that the branch is held firmly against the earth. Heap mulch over the branch at this point to a depth of 50 mm.

It is preferable to carry out this procedure in warm weather when the wood is pliable and the growth rate is rapid. Roots will eventually form at the cut and the new plant can be separated from its parent. By gently

plant can be potted into an azalea mix using a 100 mm or 125 mm container.

Few problems are likely to be experienced in propagating azaleas from cuttings. Probably the worst mistake that can be made is to keep the medium too wet. A good watering once a week is usually sufficient. If in doubt, allow the surface of the mix to dry out before the next watering. On the other hand under

Layering—a cut is made in the underside of a low-growing branch which is then pinned to the ground with a wire staple and covered with mulch.

scraping the mulch away it will be seen whether the roots are forming. Return the mulch if they are insufficiently developed—a root ball the size of a golf ball is desirable. It is a slow procedure, however, and it may take up to 12 months before the new plant can be separated from its parent, at which time it can be planted in the same manner as any other azalea.

Propagating decidous azaleas

Cuttings from deciduous azaleas do not root as freely as their evergreen cousins, and take considerably longer to achieve a sizeable root ball. Because they are so easy to grow from seed and because the seed is fairly true to the parent plant, seed propagation is the more commonly used method of propagation.

When propagating deciduous azaleas by seed, the first step is to prepare a seedling mix. This is a mixture of 3 parts river sand and 1 part peat. The river sand should be well washed to remove mud and silt. Mix the two ingredients, ensuring the peat is not pulverised but remains in a crumbled form in the mixture. Firm the mixture into pots or seed trays within 3 to 4 cm of the top of the pot and water to settle. Crumble some additional peat and moisten thoroughly, then spread to a depth of about 1 cm across the top of the sand/peat mixture.

Sprinkle the seed sparsely over the top and press down with the palm of the hand so that the seed is embedded in the moist peat. The peat should be kept moist until germination takes place, either by using an atomiser or a garden spayer that can be adjusted to spray a fine mist.

Keep the containers in a shaded position. As the seedlings begin to emerge the amount of water can be increased to a fine sprinkle to make sure that the underlying seedling mixture is kept moist.

When the plants reach a height of 5 to 7 cm they should be carefully lifted and potted into 75 to 100 mm pots using an azalea potting mix. The seed will usually germinate eratically so the seedlings will have to be lifted over a period of several weeks as they attain the required height for handling.

After potting, keep the plants in a shaded position and water regularly to ensure that they are kept growing vigorously. If the potting mix does not contain fertiliser, then one month after planting a small quantity of 8–9 month slow release fertiliser should be placed on the surface. About $1/4$ of a level teaspoon for each pot should be adequate.

6 Pests and Diseases

I will discuss the subject of pests and diseases from two angles because the home gardener and the commercial grower have different approaches to the same problems. The home gardener generally prefers to wait until there is evidence of trouble and then copes with it using simple mechanical means and avoids the use of chemicals wherever possible. The commercial grower ambushes problems using preventive measures and usually regards spraying with chemicals as the simplest operation and one which he or she has the experience, apparatus and expertise to perform expediently.

Some problems which loom large in the view of the commercial grower will not be of concern to the home gardener. Problems such as *Phytophthora* root rot and pests such as the black vine weevil should be handled by the grower so that when a home gardener makes a purchase from the retailer, he or she will receive a clean, disease-free specimen.

The Home Gardener's Approach

Foliage disfiguring pests are usually the first discerned by the gardener. These are lace bug, leaf miner and mites.

Lace bug
This is a small black-bodied insect about 3 to 4 mm long with a delicate lace-like wing pattern. It is found on the undersurface of leaves, and the first sign of damage is silvery pin pricks which show up clearly against the dark green of the leaves.

It appears to be more prevalent in NSW than in other states. The first signs occur as the weather warms and the new spring leaf growth begins to show. If left untreated by the end of the summer all leaves will be affected and become yellowish to white with a loss of vitality. At this stage nothing can be done to restore the leaves and they will eventually fall and be replaced by fresh leaves. The lesson is: early treatment will prevent this problem.

If you are prepared to spray with chemicals use Metasystox in accordance with the manufacturer's instructions. Otherwise sprays such as those based on garlic, or a dusting with derris dust may be effective and are worth trying.

Leaf miner
The damage is caused by the larvae of a small moth about 1 cm long which lays its eggs on the underside of the leaf. For the home gardener the easiest method of control is to remove those leaves which show up with a side or end of the leaf rolled under and which have a brown discolouration at this point. After removal the leaves should be burned or otherwise destroyed.

Mites
Because they are very difficult to see with the naked eye, the first sign of the presence of

mites is the mottled bronze appearance of the damaged foliage. Two sprayings of Kelthane no more than ten days apart are required to break the life-cycle.

Fungus

Fungal diseases such as petal blight and Botrytis will destroy the display of blooms if left untreated. Both result in rotting of the blooms; the obvious difference being that flowers affected by petal blight are sticky and adhere firmly to the foliage and must be manually removed, while blooms affected by Botrytis are not sticky and fall to the ground. Close examination of petal blight affected flowers after they have dried will show occasional hard, black, oval, scab-like formations about 3 or 4 mm long embedded in the surface. These are known as Sclerotia.

Botrytis seems to be more prevalent in cool autumn weather while petal blight prefers warmer weather coinciding with the mid-September flush of flowers. However, very often both diseases are present at the same time.

Chemical sprays are needed for control of both conditions and while Bayleton is most effective against petal blight it has little or no controlling action over Botrytis, just as the Botrytis or grey mould sprays will not prevent petal blight. I suggest therefore that if you elect to spray for bloom rotting generally, use a mixture of two sprays. Bayleton and Rovral, for example, are compatible and can be used in this way without damage to the plants. Delay spraying until rotting of the blooms is evident. Often two sprayings two weeks apart is all that is needed to keep the blooms fresh and unblemished.

Both diseases prefer moist, humid weather conditions for optimum development and if a dry spring is experienced it may be possible to avoid spraying. At this time watering below the foliage level is advisable, keeping the flowers as dry as possible.

It is sound management to spray at the close of the season with Bayleton to ensure the spent blooms will drop to the ground and lessen the need to manually remove dead flowers.

Other problems

If the plant is unthrifty it often shows a yellowing of the foliage with the veins a much brighter green. This can be a symptom of a number of problems. It can be due to an overly alkaline soil, iron deficiency, poor drainage, excessive watering, smothering by deep mulching, planting at too great a depth, or a heavy, clay-based, poorly drained soil. If the plant doesn't respond quickly to an application of liquid fertiliser, which would indicate a deficiency of iron or manganese, then it is advisable to investigate the other causes listed.

Often in a new azalea planting the household pet dog or cat pays it too much attention by repeatedly urinating against the plants. It may be necessary to erect a barrier to reduce these unwelcome attentions until the novelty has worn off and the new planting is accepted. In a row of plants it is often the end plant which attracts the most attention. In some cases extending the row by driving in a stake, or 'P' post as it is known by landscapers, diverts the dog's attentions from the plants to the stake.

A pest often encountered in suburban areas particularly, is the compulsive slip-nicker. Plants growing close to a footpath are most at risk from their predations but even those totally enclosed in a front garden are not entirely safe from the attentions of a determined slip-nicker. Unfortunately there is no recognised preventive measure!

The Commercial Grower's Approach

The commercial grower must anticipate problems to be overcome and work to a preventive program. First, attention must be given to the site of the operation. Azaleas are best placed on a gravel floor, preferably with a slight slope to ensure that the potted plants are not standing in surface water. Next a suitable pot (one with ample drainage holes at the base) must be selected. Then a growing medium of the desired pH, say 4.5 to 5.0, free draining and of a nature which can be replicated consistently, will be required to fill the pots.

With care taken over these details the incidence of *Phytophthora* root rot is minimised. This fungal disease should be suspected when plants show signs of wilting and the leaves begin to bronze. An examination of the root ball will reveal a brown rotting mass which breaks apart readily. There will be no sign of the white-tipped feeding roots which are normally growing from healthy plants.

When the problem does arise, treatment with granulated Ridomil manually placed on the surface soil of each container will be necessary, dosing in accordance with the manufacturer's directions.

Since the banning of DDT-based spray materials, two pests—cyclamen mite and black vine weevil—have assumed worrying proportions. Cyclamen mite damage can be recognised when growing tips show a rolling under of the leaf margins which gives the leaves the appearance of being narrower and more pointed than normal. The first signs usually occur as the weather begins to warm towards the end of October. It shows a preference for 'Pink Lace', 'White Lace', 'Duc de Rohan', 'Comtesse de Kerchove' and 'Southern Aurora', although it is not restricted to these varieties.

When an infestation is recognised, the life cycle of the mites should be broken in the early stages with two sprayings of Kelthane within ten days, and in severe infestations three sprays within fifteen days, weather permitting. As Kelthane is compatible with many other spray materials, it is advisable to incorporate a Kelthane spray with another routine spray for practical and economic reasons.

A newly released miticide, Pyranica, is receiving very favourable comments from commercial growers. It is active against eggs, nymphs and adults, and it is suggested that it be used just once each year in conjunction with the normal spray program. If mites are a problem, Pyranica may be worth trying.

The other pest to have recently become apparent is the black vine weevil. Nursery workers were mystified by the sudden loss of foliage gloss and subsequent death of increasing numbers of plants each year.

The damage is caused by the larvae of the black vine weevil and in order to combat this pest effectively it is necessary to understand its life cycle. As the name suggests, the adult is black or dark brown. It is a typical weevil in appearance, 7 to 10 mm long, with an elongated beak and rough-textured, fused wing cases which make it flightless. It is nocturnal and parthenogenic, which means that it breeds without mating. The presence of the adult is usually first recognised by its tell-tale feeding habit. It eats from the outside of the leaf, leaving a serrated or notched pattern.

The earliest hatchings of adults occur in October in the temperate regions of Australia. The weevils hatch in the soil and remain there for about three days as the shell case hardens, then they push their way out through the soil. After emergence it is at least six days before they begin to feed and a further twelve days approximately before they commence egg-laying activities, laying about six eggs per night. It is at this stage, as they start feeding and before egg-laying begins, that the spray program must be commenced for optimum effectiveness.

Orthene sprayed in accordance with the manufacturer's directions every two weeks will control the adults. If the weather forecast is unfavourable, spray earlier rather than delay the spraying. Orthene is incompatible with most other sprays so it becomes a time-consuming and costly practice. Because the emergence of adults is erratic it is essential to maintain the program until the end of February.

Once eggs are laid it is much more difficult and expensive to attack the larvae in the soil. The larvae feed on the growing tips of the roots while in their early stages of growth and the plants appear able to cope with this attack. It is in the autumn as the grubs attain a length of about 1 cm and approach the pre-pupal stage that they concentrate their attentions on the bark just at and below the soil surface, completely ringbarking the shrub and causing irreparable damage.

Where the black vine weevil has been a problem it is advisable to maintain this program religiously for two years, after which time it could be slackened off. Even so, it will still be necessary to strictly monitor the crop for signs of 'notching', or to conduct regular torchlight examination two hours after dark for signs of the adults' presence.

Other well-known pests and diseases can be kept under control using the program outlined above. Septoria spot, which can be recognised by purple and black leaf spots, and dieback, although not specifically targeted, can be kept to a minimum by the fungicides used for other purposes.

Precautions When Spraying

Before spraying plants it is advisable, particularly in the case of the home gardener with limited experience, to check with the Department of Agriculture or other authority in your state, to ensure the proposed procedure is correct. Garden centres are also happy to advise in these circumstances.

Keep in mind that the spray material may be toxic, especially in the concentrated form before dilution with water, and should be handled with extreme care, avoiding contact with any parts of the body.

Protective clothing should be used together with rubber gloves and a face mask; avoid breathing in fumes. If possible spray in the morning or evening when the air is less turbulent.

Read the information provided on the label and follow the instructions meticulously.

Only mix chemicals together when you have ensured that they are compatible. Use reliable apparatus maintained in good condition.

After spraying do not smoke, eat or drink before thoroughly washing. When storing chemicals keep them in a storage place inaccessible to children. Don't keep unlabelled chemicals indefinitely and certainly do not transfer chemicals to a bottle or jar which would normally hold foodstuffs. Empty containers should be disposed of with care.

Commercial Spray Program

Month	Possible Pests and Diseases	Symptoms	Treatment
January	Cyclamen mite	Rolling under of leaf margins, giving the leaves a smaller, narrower, more pointed appearance. Affects new growth mainly.	Kelthane, Mavrick, or on hot days, Omite.
	Two-spotted mite	Foliage shows bronze discolouration on underside. Mite can be seen with the naked eye or with the assistance of a low-powered magnifying glass.	Same as above. This should be repeated at two-weekly intervals.
	Black vine weevil	Tell-tale notching of leaves or torch-light examination two hours after dark will reveal presence of adults.	Orthene every two weeks; not to be used in mixtures.
February	Cyclamen mite	Rolling under of leaf margins	See entry for January
	Two-spotted mite	Bronze discolouration on leaf undersides	See entry for January
	Black vine weevil	Notching of leaves	See entry for January
March	Botrytis	Rotting of blooms	Bayleton plus Benlate, Daconil or Rovral
	Petal blight	Rotting of blooms	As above
April	Botrytis	Rotting of blooms	Benlate, Daconil or Rovral
	Small slugs	Chewing of blooms	Baysol
May	Botrytis	Rotting of blooms	Benlate, Daconil or Rovral
June/July	Careful watch necessary, but few problems at this time		
August	Botrytis	Rotting of blooms	Bayleton plus Benlate, Daconil or Rovral. With the onset of blooming routine fortnightly spraying should commence and be maintained until after blooming has finished.
	Petal blight	Rotting of blooms	As above
September	Botrytis	Rotting of blooms	As above
	Petal blight	Rotting of blooms	As above
October	Petal blight	Rotting of blooms	As above
	Botrytis	Rotting of blooms	As above
	Black vine weevil	Notching of leaves	Orthene every two weeks
	Leaf miner	Rolling of leaves	Orthene
	Lace bug	Silver pin holes in leaves	As above
November	Black vine weevil	Notching of leaves	As above
	Leaf miner	Rolling of leaves	As above
	Lace bug	Silver pin holes in leaves	As above
	Cyclamen mite	Rolling under of leaves	Kelthane, Mavrik, or on hot days, Omite. Spray fortnightly until end of February.
	Two-spotted mite	Bronze discolouration on leaf underside	As above
December	As above	As above	As above

7 New Varieties

If the nineteenth century was the era of the plant hunters, the twentieth century has been that of the plant breeders. Many of the exciting new azaleas that have become available in the last hundred years have been the work of hybridisers.

The Japanese were the first to venture into breeding azaleas but there have been many other patient growers who have carried out this work for love rather than money.

One of the most influential breeders, Anthony Waterer, has already been mentioned. He began growing some of the deciduous Belgian azaleas in his nursery at Knap Hill in the 1860s. He certainly was not interested in making money out of his azaleas because right up until the 1920s the Waterer family continued to grow the plants for their own pleasure and gave only a tiny proportion of them to favoured customers. One of these honoured customers was Lionel de Rothschild, who developed the Exbury range.

Both the Knap Hill and Exbury azaleas were lucky to survive the ravages of the Second World War but, fortunately, the work of their owners had inspired a post war generation of breeders in both the old and new world.

In New Zealand, Edgar Stead of Christchurch developed the Exbury stock and concentrated particularly on a fine range of red, orange and yellow shades. They were called Ilam azaleas and, after Edgar Stead's death, his work was continued by Dr J.G. Yeates, a lecturer in botany.

In recent years, the breeding of deciduous azaleas has almost come to a standstill for two main reasons. First, deciduous azaleas are a little difficult to grow from cuttings and, secondly, they grow easily from seed and are relatively true to type. Most growers concentrate on producing unnamed seedlings that flower in a delightful range of colours.

Instead the focus of attention in the twentieth century has shifted towards the hybridising of evergreen azaleas. In Japan, breeders crossed the Gumpo azalea derived from *Rhododendron eriocarpum* with other evergreen azaleas and developed the large-flowered Satsukis. They were taken further by an American, Ben Morrison, at Glenn Dale, Maryland, who used the Satsukis extensively to breed a range of evergreen azaleas with increased cold-hardiness. Two other Americans, Bobbink and Atkins, extended the Belgian-Indica hybrids and produced well-known cultivars, such as 'L.J. Bobbink' and 'Rose Queen', which are collectively known as Rutherford hybrids.

In Australia a few dedicated growers have carried out successful breeding programs. Jack Greentree of Kingsgrove (near Sydney) was a keen amateur who died in 1988 but greatly enriched the azalea scene during his lifetime. His most famous hybrid is 'Jean Alexandra'.

Fred Lovegrove, another amateur grower, crossed 'Gloria' with 'Schryderii' to combine the characteristic frilling of Gloria's bloom with the perfume of 'Schryderii'. 'Schryderii' has a very hairy leaf which is thought to give it improved disease resistance.

George Taylor of Burbank Nurseries in Wyong, NSW, has followed the lead of his boyhood hero, the American plant breeder Luther Burbank, and devoted his life to breeding new plants. Almost fifty years ago he established a nursery and began growing his 'Wonder Breed' of azaleas. The first of these, 'Silver Anniversary', is still one of the most popular but other varieties are also well known. Many of them were developed from an American import named 'Gretel'.

Through the 1980s and into the 1990s we have seen many varieties new to Australia appear on the market. These have been bred overseas—largely in Holland and the United States—and have been imported into Australia for propagation here and eventually for retail sale. Because our climatic conditions vary in so many respects from their northern hemisphere homes the performance of these plants is sometimes below expectations and their appeal is limited. Many have not had the anticipated impact on our markets.

Breeding Azaleas

In NSW, at a lovely Central Coast site an hour's drive from Sydney, is a plant breeding nursery named Paradise Plants. The proprietor, Bob Cherry, has been breeding azaleas as well as many other species, first at Gosford commencing in 1964, and then subsequently from 1972 at Kulnura. In this period he estimates that he has bred 70 000 new azaleas but considers that only twenty of these have sound commercial possibilities, with ten now in production.

Bob commenced with varieties known to be hardy under Australian conditions and exhibiting such characteristics as leaf hairiness, which deters insect pests, and flowers with thicker, waxy petals to offer more resistance to petal blight.

The characteristics he considers of paramount importance when assessing new plants are:

1. Garden worthiness: this includes such features as vigour under Australian conditions, competitiveness with other species, growth habit and general appearance of the plant.
2. Flowering habit: extended flowering period ultimately achieving year round blooming.
3. Double flowers with the growth habit of the old-fashioned single varieties.
4. Clustered blooms with a rhododendron-like inflorescence.
5. Some sun tolerance.
6. Scent.

The breeding cycle commences with the selection of the two parents. Many double flowers have incomplete or sterile male components, but have sound female parts, so that consideration is given to which will be the seed-bearing variety and which will provide the pollen. The introduction of pollen to the receptive female plant is carried out manually in the spring of the first year of the project. The flowers pollinated in this fashion are carefully identified and details of the two parents recorded.

In the autumn of year two, the seed capsules are collected, again recorded and identified, and stored for complete drying out. The seed of azaleas is very small, like ground pepper in appearance, and each capsule can contain many hundreds of seeds. In the spring of the same year these seeds are sown into a seed-growing mixture and germinated. When the seedlings reach an appropriate size they are carefully lifted and planted individually into small tubes. The recording and identification processes are repeated.

By the spring of the third year they have reached sufficient size to be potted into 125 mm pots.

In the spring of the fourth year—three years from the time of pollination—the first flowers will be seen. Usually about 30% will flower at this time, and evaluation of the flowers can be undertaken. Absolute ruthlessness must be exhibited in this procedure—any plants failing in any of the criteria must be discarded.

By the spring of the fifth year 90% of the plants will have flowered and the remaining unflowered plants are discarded.

Cross-pollinating the parent plants in spring. The breeder is holding the female flower in his left hand; the pollen-bearing male plant is held in the right hand. The petals on the male plant are torn off to expose the anthers. The pollen is then manually dusted on to the receptive (i.e. sticky) stigma on the female flower.

The seedling offspring, 18 months after cross-pollination of the parent plants. The seedlings are highly variable and will take between 1 and 3 years to develop flowers.

Of the hundreds of plants that germinated only a handful will remain at this stage, even though the evaluation has been based on flower appearance only. Now comes the assessment of all the other necessary factors. The bloom timing, growth habit, height to which it will grow and sun tolerance, can only be determined by growing the selected plants for a further two or three years.

Plant Variety Rights

Prior to the introduction of Plant Variety Rights Legislation in the late 1980s a breeder could introduce and market a new variety, but then lost any exclusive rights to it. Other nurseries having obtained stock could use it for propagation and sell the resulting plants without any acknowledgment of the original breeder.

The production and marketing of a new variety is a long, time-consuming, arduous process deserving monetary reward. It requires meticulous identification in all phases of development.

Let us assume that one plant has passed all the tests and is considered worthy of marketing. It is at this stage that the breeder must protect the investment of time, labour and costs using the provisions of the Plant Variety Rights Act.

12 months later the tubed seedlings are ready for potting into 125 mm pots.

The Plant Variety Rights Office undertakes to have the plants examined for three qualities: Distinction, Uniformity and Stability; known as DUS qualities. For this purpose the applicant is allocated an 'accredited qualified person' who acts as a consultant during all phases of the testing process.

A trial is set up to show how the new testing variety compares with say two well-known similar varieties, in a predetermined series of plant features. In the case of azaleas the compared features could be flower colour, form, size and timing, leaf size, colour, shape and hairiness, and growth habit. Where the parentage is known the two parent plants would seem to be ideal for comparison.

Ten plants of each of the varieties in appropriately sized containers are placed alongside one another and grown and observed at regular intervals for as long as it takes to establish the elements of DUS.

In the case of azaleas it would need a complete growth cycle of twelve months. If at the end of this time the DUS elements indicate a positive result, the breeder applies for Plant Variety Rights over the new cultivar. If the accredited person supports the application then the PVR examining committee is likely to grant the request.

With the granting of PVR the breeder is acknowledged as the creator of the variety, names it and must now market it successfully to take advantage of the ownership.

The next important step is to build the numbers of plants to the level which will make the plant available to buyers. Vegetative propagation from cuttings is a slow process but in this modern age plant multiplication can be greatly accelerated by the technique of tissue culture.

The responsibility for making a financial success of the venture rests with the owner, and he or she has to exercise skills in advertising and promotion, something that was probably unthought of when the male and female azaleas were matched several years earlier.

Having brought the product to the attention of the nursery industry, the breeder may arrange for licensed growers in the other states to sell to local markets on the breeder's behalf. They will be provided with plant material, probably in the form of tubed stock for ease of transportation, promotional material and labels for which they will pay an agreed price. In subsequent years they will probably grow their own plants from the original stock, acknowledging the breeder by returning a royalty for each plant sold.

The process is quite expensive and this in itself ensures that inferior plants are not likely to be promoted.

Importing plants covered by Plant Variety Rights

When an Australian nursery is interested in importing a variety covered by PVR from overseas, negotiations are made through the local PVR office. The holder of the PVR overseas sends an authorisation to the importer in Australia, on the receipt of which an application is made to the PVR office in Australia. This establishes the identity of the variety with photographs and precise botanical descriptions against which the plant material is inspected on arrival in Australia. The cost of establishing the rights is approximately $4000 including photography.

The local holder of the PVR undertakes to record all plants sold and return to the breeder the royalties payable. This procedure represents a considerable exercise in accountancy and record keeping and is not without cost. This itself is an insurance that imported species must be quality plants with high market potential.

8 The Azalea Grower's Calendar

January

Having allowed time to recover from the excesses of the festive season, examine your azaleas for the presence of leaf miner and lace bug. If they are present take the appropriate remedial action (see chapter on 'Pests and Diseases'). As the weather should be warm to hot at this time of the year, regular watering will be necessary. A liquid feed application should be made at some time during the month. Tip pruning where necessary will complete the month's operations.

February

Plants should be growing vigorously by now and responding to the regular watering and liquid feeding. New growth will be forming at the points where tip pruning has been carried out.

March

In this month you should see some spot bloom on the doubles and on the long-flowering varieties an autumn show of colour can be expected. Inspect blooms for damage by small slugs on cool moist mornings and after rain. If damage occurs apply snail bait around the plants, taking the necessary precautions to prevent pets from feeding on it. Tip pruning, liquid fertilising and watering are ongoing activities.

April

Discontinue tip pruning. If you are experiencing rainy conditions it is likely that the autumn spot blooms will not be holding for any length of time. If this is the case, close inspection will possibly reveal rotting of the bloom, giving a mushy appearance at the base of the flower. You may also find browning of the buds when they get to the colouring stage. This condition is likely to be Botrytis, or 'grey mould' as it is commonly known, and is often mistaken for petal blight. Spray according to instructions under 'Pests and Diseases—Botrytis'.

May

Plant growth is slowing down and spring buds are starting to set. Make this month's liquid fertilising the last before September. You may notice that leaves are dropping and forming a mat beneath the plants. This is normal as evergreen azaleas continually shed and replace leaves. Watering may be reduced but not neglected.

June

Plants will have slowed down and will not require much attention.

July

In frost-susceptible areas it is common for the leaves to burn after heavy frosts. This reveals itself as a dark brown discolouration of the new tip growth. It is not a disaster—although the burnt area will probably fall away, usually within a fortnight, new shoots will soon begin to show. Nature has simply given you a helping hand with the pruning. In areas where frosts are experienced, damage can be minimised by keeping the foliage as dry as possible. In other words, don't water the foliage in the evening if you suspect that frosts may be present next morning. Watering in the morning while the frost is present and before the sun shines on the plants is effective. If the plants are in semi-shaded areas frosts should only form in extreme conditions.

August
Take your annual holidays.

September
Flowering is now in full swing. Take time to sit in the garden and admire the display which is the reward for your persistence with this program. If petal blight raises its ugly head a spraying with Bayleton will correct the problem. It will usually occur in the aftermath of a period of rain. Although azaleas in full bloom require plenty of moisture, endeavour to water beneath the plants and keep the flowers as dry as possible.

October
In the first week, weather permitting, spray with Bayleton to ensure that any blooms affected by petal blight will drop off and not adhere to the plants as this interferes with new growth developing from the bloom sites. Include in this spray a general purpose insecticide such as Supracide to discourage leaf miner and lace bug. Manually remove any dead flowers that have not fallen from the plant.

Towards the end of the month spread long-term fertiliser under the plants and cover with a well-rotted mulch of animal manure or compost. Remember that mulch should not be so deep that it smothers the plant. Commence the liquid fertilising program.

November
Tip prune, keep watering regularly, and continue liquid fertilising.

December
Water regularly, liquid feed and tip prune. This is the time to take cuttings if propagation is considered.

Above: Three varieties of Mollis azaleas.
Below: Azaleas are ideal plants for the semi-shaded garden.

Above: Pink and white spring flower display featuring azaleas (middle), accompanied by primulas (foreground), camellia (rear left) and magnolia (rear right).

'Alba Magna'

'Alphonse Anderson'

'Alba Magna' standard

'Ambrosius'

'Beverley Haerens'

'Anna Kehr'

'Bride's Bouquet'

'California Peach'

'Centenary Heritage'

'Christmas Cheer'

'Comtesse de Kerchove'

'Coral Wings'

'Dancer'

'Elsa Karga'

'Emily Knights'

'Eri Schame'

'Eureka'

'Fairy Bells'

'Fairy Queen'

'Festival Queen'

'Fred Colbert'

'Garden Party'

'Glowing Embers'

'Goyet'

'Happy Days'

'Jean Alexandra'

'Jennifer Ann'

'Kalimna Pearl'

'Kasane Kagaribi'

'Kirin'

'Lucille 'K'

'Madonna'

'Maves'

'Mission Bells'

'Mrs Gerda Kint'

'My Fair Lady'

'Neil Armstrong'

'Nuccio's Dewdrops'

'Only One Earth'

'Orange Delight'

'Orchidflora'

'Paradise Coconut Ice'

'Paradise Honey'

'Paradise Fiesta'

'Paradise Sensuous'

'Paul Schame'

'Peach Blossom'

'Phil Sherringham'

'Phryne'

'Pink Dream'

'Red Poppy'

'Redwing'

'Ripples'

'Rosa Belton'

'Rosa Lee'

'Rosalie'

'Rose King'

'Rose Magnifica'

'Rose Queen'

'Saidee Kirk'

'Seraphim'

'Silver Anniversary'

'Snowflake'

'Snow Prince'

'Southern Aurora'

'Special Occasion'

'Splendens'

'Starlight'

'Sui-Yohi'

'Sweet Nellie'

'Teena Maree'

'The Teacher'

'Thelma Bray'

'Trisha Tilly'

'Versicolour'

'Violaceae'

'White Bouquet'

'White Schame'

'M.J. Vervane' (pink flower) showing sporting to
'Vervaneana rubra' (red flower)

43

'White Prince' reverting to 'Rose Queen'

Gumpo azaleas

Lace bug damage—early stage

Lace bug damage—advanced stage

Petal blight

Frost damage

Yellow leaves are an indication that the plant is suffering from a nutrient deficiency.

Leaf yellowing (chlorosis)

9 Descriptions of Popular Varieties

Advent Bells (Indica) Medium height. Bright red, bell-shaped, semi-double flowers borne in clusters. Spot blooms in autumn; peak flowering in spring.

Ailine (Hybrid) Medium height; bushy growth. Large white double blooms. Long flowering, sun tolerant.

Alba Magnifica (Southern Indica) Tall growing. Single fragrant white blooms. Hardy. Mid-season blooming.

Albert Elizabeth (Indica) Medium height. Double white flowers with rose edging and frilled tendency. Mid-season blooming.

Alphonse Anderson (Southern Indica) Tall growing. Single pink flowers, edged with white; darker rose throat. Hardy. Mid-season blooming.

Amaghasa (Satsuki) Medium height; spreading growth. Bright salmon-red, single. Late flowering.

Ambrosius (Indica) Medium height; spreading bushy growth. Dark carmine, double. Spot flowering in autumn; free early spring blooming.

Anna Kehr (Hybrid) Above medium height; upright vigorous growth. Candy pink, full formal double. Mid-season flowering.

Avenir (Indica) Medium height; bushy growth. Large, brick red, double. Spot flowers in autumn; peak flowering in early spring.

Azuma Kagami (Kurume) Tall bushy growth. Dark pink with lighter centre, semi-double hose-in-hose. Mid-season flowering.

Ballerina (Indica) Below medium height; compact growth. Creamy-white double with frilled cyclamen edging. Late flowering.

Balsaminaeflora (Indica) Low, spreading, compact growth. Salmon, very full double. Spot blooms in early autumn; peak flowering in late spring. Self layering.

Beatrix (Indica) Medium height; spreading growth. Salmon-orange, double. Spot flowers from autumn; peak flowering in early spring. Sport of Paul Schame.

Bertina (Indica) Medium height; bushy growth. Large, salmon-pink, single. Spot flowers in autumn; peak flowering in mid-spring.

Betty Cuthbert (Kurume) Medium height; bushy growth. Small, pale pink hose-in-hose. Shiny foliage. Mid-season blooming.

Beverley Haerens (Indica) Medium height; bushy growth. The large double flowers are white in spring but shell pink at other times of the year. Spot flowers in autumn; main flush early in spring. Blooms need protection from strong wind. Sport of Avenir.

Bonnie McKee (Indica) Medium height; bushy growth. Large, deep mauve, double. Early to mid-season flowering.

Bride's Bouquet (Kerrigan Hybrid) Medium height; upright growth. White, formal double. Delicate blooms need protection from direct sunlight and strong winds. Mid-season flowering.

California Peach (Indica) Medium height; bushy growth. Large, peach-pink, double. Spot flowers in autum; peak flowering in early spring. Sport of Avenir.

Charlie (Indica Hybrid) Low compact growth. Often has untidy appearance. Purplish-pink, double. Long-flowering, from autumn to late spring. Sport of Lucie.

Centenary Heritage (Indica) Spreading bushy growth. Salmon-pink hose-in-hose clusters. Mid-season to late flowering.

Christmas Cheer (Kurume) Low compact growth. Small, bright carmine-red, single hose-in-hose. Some spot blooms in autumn; a blaze of colour in spring.

Christmas Pink (Indica) Low spreading growth. Pale mauve-pink, double. Flowers from autumn to spring. Definitely one for the connoisseur because it is not a strong competitor.

Comtesse De Kerchove (Indica) Medium height; bushy growth. Soft opal pink muted to white on petal tips, double. Early spring blooming.

Coral Wings (Indica Hybrid) Dense compact growth. Salmon hose-in-hose. The outer petals are irregular and imperfectly formed. Hardy. Spot flowers in autumn; peak display in early to mid-spring. Sport of Redwing.

Dancer (Indica) Medium height; bushy growth. Salmon-pink, semi-double hose-in-hose. Hardy. Spot flowers in autumn; peak display in mid-spring.

Desert Rose (Indica Hybrid) Medium height. Salmon-pink with red throat, semi-double. Spot flowers in early autumn; mid-spring flush.

Dogwood (Hybrid) Medium height; bushy growth. Small, narrow, red blooms with white edges. Sun tolerant. Late flowering.

Dogwood Red (Hybrid) Medium height; bushy growth. Small red blooms. Sun tolerant. Late flowering.

Dogwood White (Hybrid) Medium height; bushy growth. Small white blooms. Sun tolerant. Late flowering.

Dr Arnold (Indica) Medium height; bushy growth. Large, rose-pink, single. Long flowering, from autumn to early spring. Hardy. Sport of Pink Dream.

Dr Bergmann (Indica) Medium height; upright growth. Bright orange-red paling towards the centre, dark throat, semi-double. Dark green glossy foliage. Spot flowers in autumn; peak display in early spring.

Duc de Rohan (Southern Indica) Tall compact growth. Bright salmon blooms with rose throat, single. Hardy. Mid to late spring flowering.

Elizabeth Lawrence (Southern Indica) Tall bushy growth. Violet single blooms. Hardy. Early to mid-season blooming.

Elsa Karga (Indica) Medium height; bushy growth. Bright red, double blooms. Early to mid-season flowering.

Emily Knights (Kurume) Tall, vigorous, bushy growth. Bright red, star-shaped single blooms. Hardy.

Flowers mid-season.

Eri Schame (Indica) Medium height; bushy growth. Bright salmon-pink blooms edged with white, semi-double. Flowers from autumn to spring. Sport of Paul Schame.

Esmeralda (Kurume) Tall, vigorous, bushy growth. Small, pink, single blooms. Mid-season flowering.

Eureka (Indica) Low, compact, bushy growth. Cyclamen-pink with white margins, single. Long flowering, from autumn to spring.

Exquisite (Southern Indica) Tall, vigorous, spreading growth. Lilac-pink with red throat, single. Frgrant. Flowers mid-season. Sport of Magnifica.

Fairy Bells (Kurume) Tall, vigorous, bushy growth. Pale pink flecked with darker pink, cream throat. Long flowering, from autumn to spring.

Fairy Queen (Kurume) Medium height; bushy growth. Light pink, semi-double hose-in-hose. Mid-season blooming.

Festival Queen (Indica) Upright vigorous growth. Large, white, semi-double. Late flowering.

Fielder's White (Southern Indica) Medium height; spreading bushy growth. White blooms with greenish-yellow throat, single, fragrant. Mid-season flowering.

Flamingo (Hybrid) Medium height; bushy growth. Purple double blooms. Sun tolerant. Long flowering.

Fred Colbert (Kurume Hybrid) Compact bushy growth. Bright red, semi-double hose-in-hose. Mid-season flowering.

Garden Party (Hybrid) Vigorous bushy growth. Rose-pink, semi-double hose-in-hose. Long flowering, from autumn to spring.

Geisha Girl (Satsuki Hybrid) Medium height; spreading growth. Single blooms varying from bright cyclamen pink with white throat, to blooms that are all cyclamen pink. Late blooming.

Glowing Embers (Hybrid Kurume) Medium height; vigorous growth. Bright orange-red blooms with pointed petals, semi-double. Mid-season blooming.

Goyet (Indica) Above medium height; open bushy growth. Large, bright red double. Some autumn blooms; peak flowering in mid-spring.

Gretel (Indica) Low compact growth. White with

dark cyclamen frilled edges, double. Mid to late spring flowering.

Guanda Pink (Hybrid)   Low bushy growth. Large, apricot-pink, double. Long flowering.

Guanda Red (Hybrid)   Low bushy growth. Cerise, double. Long flowering.

Gumpo Petunia (Dwarf)   Dense low spreading growth to 50 cm. Pink, frilled, single blooms with white edges. Small leaves. Late flowering.

Gumpo Pink (Dwarf)   Dense low spreading growth to 35 cm. Pale pink, frilled, single blooms. Small leaves. Late flowering.

Gumpo Salmon (Dwarf)   Dense low spreading growth to 35 cm. Salmon-pink, frilled, single blooms. Small leaves. Late flowering.

Gumpo Stripe (Dwarf)   Dense low spreading growth to 50 cm. White with mauve flecks and segments, single. Small leaves. Late flowering.

Gumpo White (Dwarf)   Dense low spreading growth to 35 cm. White, frilled, single blooms. Small leaves. Late flowering.

Happy Days (Indica hybrid)   Above medium height; vigorous bushy growth. Light purple, double hose-in-hose. Long flowering, from autumn to spring.

Hatsu No Hana (Satsuki)   Dense bushy spreading growth. Single blooms varying from white with salmon-red stripes to completely salmon-red. Late blooming.

Helmut Vogel (Hybrid)   Medium height; bushy growth. Cerise, double. Long flowering.

Higasa (Satsuki)   Spreading open growth. Large rose-pink blooms with darker throat. Late blooming.

Inga (Hybrid)   Medium height; bushy growth. White edged with pink, double. Long flowering. Sport of Helmut Vogel.

Issho No Haru (Satsuki)   Bushy spreading growth. Single blooms, varying from white flushed with mauve with darker mauve stripe, to all purple. Late blooming.

James Belton (Indica x Schryderii)   Above medium height; bushy growth. Pale pink with lavender throat, single. Spot blooms in autumn; peak flowering in mid-spring.

Janique (Hybrid)   Tall bushy growth. Large, orange-red, double. Long flowering. Hardy.

Jean Alexandra (Southern Indica)   Tall bushy growth. Pale pink single to semi-double blooms. Early to mid-season flowering.

Jennifer Ann (Indica)   Medium height; bushy growth. White double blooms. Fragrant. Spot blooms in autumn; peak flowering in mid-spring.

Jill Seymour (Kurume)   Medium bushy growth. Pink with red stripes, semi-double. Mid-season blooming.

Kalimna Pearl (Indica)   Tall vigorous bushy growth. Light lavender-pink blooms with intensified colour in the centre, double. Mid-season blooming. Sport of Alphonse Anderson.

Kasane Kagaribi (Kurume)   Low dense spreading growth. Dark reddish-salmon with a pale salmon-pink throat, single. Mid-season flowering.

Kirin (Kurume)   Medium height; bushy growth. Silvery rose-pink, hose-in-hose. Long flowering, from autumn to spring.

Kosmos (Hybrid)   Medium height; bushy growth. Large, cerise, double. Hardy. Long flowering.

Little Red Riding Hood (Kurume)   Compact growth. Orange-red, single. Mid-season flowering.

L.J. Bobbink (Rutherford Hybrid)   Above medium height; bushy growth. Lavender blooms paling to white centre, semi-double hose-in-hose. Late flowering.

Lucie (Indica Hybrid)   Compact low growth. Rose-pink, double. Long flowering, from autumn to late spring.

Lucille 'K' (Indica Hybrid)   Low, bushy, vigorous growth. Single hose-in-hose blooms, the outer petals being imperfectly developed, and inner petals pointed red with a fine white line around the edge. Long flowering, from autumn to spring. Sport of Redwing.

Madame Auguste Haerens (Indica)   Medium height; bushy growth. Coral-pink with darker centre and white margins, double. Autumn spot flowering; peak display in early spring. Sport of Avenir.

Madam Butterfly (Indica)   Tall vigorous bushy growth. Mauve with intensified colour in the centre, double. Mid-season blooming. Sport of Alphonse Anderson.

Madam Van Ackers (Indica)   Medium height; bushy growth. Cerise, pea-shaped double blooms. Spot flowering; peak display in early spring.

Madonna (Indica)   Medium height; bushy growth. White, semi-double. Large leaves. Mid-season flowering.

Magnifica (Southern Indica)   Tall vigorous sprawling growth. Rose-violet single blooms with subtle fragrance. Mid-season flowering.

Mardi Gras (Indica)   Compact bushy growth. Red, ruffled, single blooms with white edges. Spot flowering from autumn; peak display in mid-spring.

Martha Gardner (Indica)   Compact bushy growth. Spanish red, double. Long flowering, from autumn to spring.

Maves (Indica)   Tall but slow growing bushy shrub. Clear bright red, single, often with centre petaloids. Flowers mid-season.

Mission Bells (Hybrid)   Medium height; bushy growth. Brilliant red, ruffled, semi-double. Spot flowers from autumn; peak flowering in mid-spring.

Mrs Gerda Kint (Indica)   Low compact dense growth. Pink with white edges and darker centre, single. Small pointed leaves. Spot flowers from autumn; peak flowering in mid-spring.

Mrs Gerda Kint Alba (Indica)   Low compact bushy growth. White, single. Mid-spring blooms. Sport of Mrs Gerda Kint.

My Fair Lady (Indica)   Medium height; bushy growth. Bright coral-pink with wide white border and darker centre. Spot flowers in autumn; main flush early in spring. Sport of Beverley Haerens.

Nancy Marie (Hybrid)   Tall bushy growth. Small, white, single with star-shaped red centre. Sun hardy. Late flowering. Sport of Dogwood.

Neil Armstrong (Indica)   Above medium height; open bushy growth. Spanish red, large, double. Spot flowering in autumn; peak display in spring. Sport of Goyet.

Nuccio's Dewdrops (Hybrid)   Below medium height; compact bushy growth. Blush pink to white with rose-pink spotted throat and greenish centre. Single to semi-double. Late spring blooming.

Only One Earth (Indica)   Medium height; bushy growth. Bright cerise, semi-double. Early spring flowering.

Orange Chimes (Indica)   Medium height; bushy growth. Orange, semi-double bell-shaped flowers borne in clusters. Spot flowers from autumn to spring. Flowers are very tender and must be protected from wind and sun. Sport of Advent Bells.

Orange Delight (Hybrid)   Below medium height; compact vigorous growth. Large, bright orange, single. Some spot flowering from autumn; peak display in late spring.

Orchidflora (Indica)   Medium height; bushy growth can tend to become straggly, so needs attention to pruning. Large, mauve-pink, semi-double. Long flowering with early spring flush.

Orchidflora Alba (Indica)   Large, white, semi-double. Sport of Orchidflora—same comments apply.

Orchidflora Pink (Indica)   Pale pink blooms edged with white. Sport of Orchidflora—same comments apply.

Orchidflora Salmon (Indica)   Large, bright salmon-pink blooms. Sport of Orchidflora—same comments apply.

Osaraku (Kurume)   Medium height; bushy growth. Soft lavender fading to white throat, single. Mid-season blooming.

Osta (Hybrid)   Medium height; bushy growth. Large, white with pink blotch, single. Spot flowers in autumn; peak display in mid-spring. Sport of Bertina.

Osta Red (Hybrid)   Medium height; bushy growth. Large, red, single blooms. Spot flowers in autumn; peak display in mid spring. Sport of Osta.

Paloma (Hybrid)   Medium height; bushy growth. White double flowers. Long flowering. Sport of Helmut Vogel.

Paradise Charity (Hybrid)   Medium height; bushy growth. Soft pink, double. Long flowering and sun tolerant.

Paradise Coconut Ice (Hybrid)   Bushy vigorous growth. Large, two-tone pink, double blooms. Mid-season flowering.

Paradise Elfin (Kurume)   Bushy growth. Salmon, hose-in-hose. Sun tolerant. Mid-season flowering.

Paradise Fiesta (Hybrid)   Vigorous bushy growth. White with pink stripes, single to semi-double. Sun tolerant. Long flowering.

Paradise Honey (Hybrid)   Upright bushy growth. White with honey coloured throat, scented, single. Sun tolerant.

Paradise Pixie (Kurume)   Bushy growth. Small, rose-pink, hose-in-hose. Sun tolerant. Mid-season flowering.

Paradise Radiance (Hybrid)   Medium height; bushy growth. Deep rose-pink, hose-in-hose. Sun tolerant. Mid-season flowering.

Paradise Sensuous (Hybrid)   Upright bushy growth. Rose-lavender, scented, double. Sun tolerant. Long flowering.

Paradise Suzie (Hybrid)   Medium height; bushy growth. Blush pink blooms with darker throat. Sun tolerant. Long-flowering.

Paradise Voodoo (Hybrid)   Medium height; bushy growth. Orange-red, hose-in-hose. Long flowering.

Pauline Mardner (Indica)   Medium height; bushy growth. Long-petalled, bright pink, semi-double. Long flowering, from autumn to mid-spring.

Paul Schame (Indica)   Medium height; bushy growth. Bright salmon-red, double. Unstable, sporting freely. Long flowering, from autumn to spring.

Peach Blossom (Hybrid)   Medium height; bushy growth. Delicate, small, single blush-pink blooms. Mid-season flowering.

Petrick Alba (Indica)   Low compact shrub; slow growing. White double blooms. Early and late flowering. Poor competitor but excellent tub specimen. Often mistakenly called Madame Petrick Alba.

Phil Sherringham (Indica x Schryderii)   Above medium height; bushy growth. White to lavender double blooms. Spot flowers from autumn to mid-spring. Sport of James Belton.

Phoenicea (Phoeniceum Hybrid)   Tall bushy hardy and vigorous growth. Violet-rose, single. Mid-season flowering.

Phryne (Indica)   Medium height; bushy growth. Creamy-white, frilled, double. Mid-season flowering.

Pink Dream (Indica)   Medium height; bushy growth. Large, soft pink with darker throat, single. Hardy. Long flowering, from autumn to spring.

Pink Lace (Southern Indica)   Tall compact growth. Pink with white edge and dark throat, single. Blooms mid to late spring. Hardy. Sport of Duc de Rohan.

Pink Ruffles (Indica)   Medium bushy growth. Salmon-pink blooms edged with white, heavily ruffled, double. Long flowering, from autumn to early spring. The blooms should be kept as dry as possible for best results.

Pink Tiger (Indica Hybrid)   Tall bushy shrub. Lavender-pink with purplish red spots in throat, ruffled, single. Late flowering.

Pride of Dorking (Southern Indica)   Tall bushy growth. Carmine-red, single. Vigorous and late flowering.

Princess Maude (Amoenum Hybrid)   Medium height; vigorous bushy growth. Bright cerise, single. Hardy. Flowers mid-season.

Purple Glitters (Kurume Hybrid)   Medium height; dense bushy growth. Bright purple, single. Mid-season flowering.

Red Line (Indica)   Medium height; bushy growth. White with irregular salmon-pink speckles and small segments, double. Early and long flowering. Sport of Eri Schame.

Red Poppy (Indica Hybrid)   Medium height; bushy growth. Glowing dark red with satiny sheen, single to semi-double. Long spot blooming, followed by peak display in early spring.

Red Ruffles (Indica)   Medium height; bushy growth. Heavily ruffled, deep salmon-rose, double. Long flowering, from autumn to early spring. As with Pink Ruffles, if the blooms become too wet Botrytis may become a problem.

Redwing (Indica Hybrid)   Spreading dense growth. Bright red, single hose-in-hose; the outer petals being irregular and imperfectly formed. Long flowering from autumn to spring. Early to mid-season flowering. A most versatile variety.

Ripples (Kerrigan Hybrid)   Low bushy compact growth. Ruffled, rose-red, double. Long flowering, from autumn to spring.

Rosa Belton (Indica x Schryderii)   Above medium height; bushy growth. White with bright mauve border and greenish throat, single. Long flowering, from autumn to spring.

Rosa Lee (Kurume Hybrid)   Medium height; dense bushy growth. Bright cerise, small neat hose-in-hose.

Spot flowers from autumn; peak display in mid-spring.

Rosalie (Indica)   Medium height; bushy growth. Bright mauve-pink, semi-double. Mid-season flowering.

Rose King (Rutherford Hybrid)   Above medium height; bushy growth. Deep rose-pink, semi-double. Long flowering: spot flowers from autumn; peak display in early spring. Sport of Rose Queen.

Rose Magnifica (Southern Indica)   Tall vigorous sprawling growth habit. Single rose-pink blooms with subtle fragrance. Mid-season flowering. Sport of Magnifica.

Rose Queen (Rutherford Hybrid)   Above medium height; bushy growth. Bright pink, semi-double. Spot flowers from autumn; peak flowering in early spring.

Rosina (Indica)   Medium height; upright bushy growth. Soft pink, semi-double. Mid-season flowering.

Ruth Kirk (Indica)   Medium height; bushy growth. Salmon-pink paling to white throat with greenish spots, single. Early spring blooming.

Saidee Kirk (Indica)   Vigorous bushy growth. Shell pink with lemon throat, double. Glossy leaves. Mid-season flowering.

Scarlet Gem (Kurume)   Medium height; bushy growth. Orange-scarlet blooms have a unique hose-in-hose-formation with three trumpet-shaped blooms forming one inside the other. As blooms tend to burn when exposed to direct sunlight or strong winds, a protected site is advisable. Mid-season flowering.

Schryderii (Mucronatum Hybrid)   Tall bushy growth. Single white blooms with spotted lilac throat and subtle perfume. The foliage is sticky to the touch. Spot blooming; peak flowering in mid-spring.

Schryderii Mauve (Mucronatum Hybrid)   Pale mauve with lilac throat, single. Sport of Schryderii. Other details same as Schryderii.

Searchlight (Indica)   Low bushy growth. Ruffled double white blooms; occasional blooms marked with splashes or segments of rose-pink. Long flowering from autumn to spring.

Seikai (Kurume)   Compact bushy growth. White, semi-double hose-in-hose. Mid-season flowering.

September Bells (Kurume Hybrid)   Tall bushy growth. Bright salmon-pink, bell-shaped single blooms. Late spring flowering.

Seraphim (Kurume)   Medium height; bushy growth. Pale pink with spotted throat, hose-in-hose. Mid-season flowering.

Shin-Kyo (Satsuki)   Medium height; upright bushy growth. Light salmon-pink with darker edges, single. Variations include white flowers. Late flowering.

Silver Anniversary (Indica)   Medium height; bushy growth. Pale pink with paler tips, varies from hose-in-hose to semi-double hose-in-hose. Mid-spring flowering.

Snowflake (Kurume)   Compact bushy growth. Small, white, single hose-in-hose. Mid-season flowering.

Snow Prince (Rutherford Hybrid)   Above medium height; bushy growth. White, semi-double. Spot flowers from autumn; peak flowering in early spring. Sport of Rose Queen.

Southern Aurora (Indica)   Medium height; bushy growth. Deep apricot-salmon blooms muted white, double. Early spring blooming. Sport of Comtesse de Kerchove.

Special Occasion (Hybrid)   Medium height; bushy growth. Light candy pink with lemon throat and prominent dark stamens and pistil, single. Late flowering.

Splendens (Indica)   Vigorous upright bushy growth. Bright salmon-pink with darker throat, single. Mid-season flowering.

Starlight (Kerrigan Hybrid)   Below medium height; bushy growth. Delicate double salmon-pink blooms with greenish throat. Late blooming.

Stella Maris (Hybrid)   Medium height; bushy growth. Pinkish-white, single. Mid-season flowering. Sport of Rosalie.

Sui-Yohi (Kurume)   Medium height; dense bushy growth. Flesh-coloured, flushed salmon-pink at petal edges. Incomplete hose-in-hose, the outer row of petals being bracts only. Mid-season flowering.

Sweet Nellie (Indica Hybrid)   Medium height; spreading growth. Clusters of cerise semi-double hose-in-hose blooms. Mid-season flowering.

Teena Marie (Hybrid)   Medium height; vigorous bushy growth. Bright salmon-pink, semi-double hose-in-hose. Spot flowers from autumn; mid spring flush.

Temperance (Indica)   Tall bushy growth. Mauve

semi-double blooms. Mid-season flowering.

Terra Nova (Hybrid)   Medium height; bushy growth. Baby pink double blooms. Long flowering. Sport of Helmut Vogel.

Thelma Bray (Indica)   Medium height; bushy growth. Mauve with white throat, semi-double. Mid-season blooming.

The Teacher (Indica)   Medium height; bushy growth. Pale pink blooms edged with bright rose-pink, semi-double. Flowers mid-spring.

Trisha Tilly (Kurume)   Medium height; bushy growth. Creamy-white with spotted throat, semi-double hose-in-hose. Mid-season blooming.

Versicolour (Indica)   Medium height; bushy growth. Cream double with many splashes, flecks and segments of bright salmon-pink. Long flowering, from autumn to spring. Sport of Paul Schame.

Violacea (Indica)   Below medium height; spreading growth. Deep violet, double. Spot flowers from autumn; main flush in early spring.

Violetta (Kurume)   Medium height; bushy growth. Soft violet, semi-double hose-in-hose. Flowers mid-season.

Waka Kayede (Kurume)   Above medium height; bushy growth. Bright cerise-crimson, single. Mid-season flowering.

Ward's Ruby (Kurume)   Medium height; bushy growth. Blood-red, single. Late flowering.

White Bouquet (Indica)   Medium height; bushy growth. White with green throat, semi-double. Spot flowers from autumn; early spring flush.

White Gish (Rutherford Hybrid)   Medium height; bushy growth. White, semi-double hose-in-hose. Spot flowers from autumn; mid-spring flush.

White Lace (Southern Indica)   Tall compact growth. White single blooms. Mid to late spring flowering. Sport of Duc de Rohan.

White Prince (Rutherford Hybrid)   Above medium height; bushy growth. White blooms with red spotted throat, semi-double. Spot flowers from autumn; peak flowering in early spring.

White Schame (Indica)   Medium height; bushy growth. Pure white blooms, semi-double. Long flowering, from autumn to spring. Sport of Eri Schame.

10 Summary of Popular Varieties

	FLOWER FEATURES						PLANT FEATURES			
Variety	Colour	Type	Size	Timing	Sun	Height (m)	Growth Habit	Leaf Size	Tub Culture	Hardiness
Advent Bells	Bright red	Semi-double	Med.	Spot, early	No	1	Spreading	Med.	Yes	Average
Ailine	White	Double	Large	Long	Yes	1	Bushy	Med.	Yes	Hardy
Alba Magnifica	White	Single	Med.	Mid	Yes	2	Tall spreading	Large	No	Very hardy
Albert Elizabeth	White, rose edge	Double	Med.	Mid	No	0.75	Spreading open	Med.	Yes	Low
Alphonse Anderson	Pink, white edge	Single	Med.	Mid	Yes	2	Tall spreading	Large	No	Very hardy
Amaghasa	Salmon red	Single	Very large	Late	No	1	Medium spreading	Large	Yes	Hardy
Ambrosius	Dark carmine	Double	Med.	Spot, early	No	0.75	Spreading bushy	Med.	Yes	Average
Anna Kehr	Candy pink	Full double	Med.	Mid	No	1.25	Upright bushy	Med.	Yes	Hardy
Avenir	Brick red	Double	Large	Spot, early	No	1	Spreading bushy	Med.	Yes	Average
Azuma Kagami	Dark pink	Semi-double hose-in-hose	Small to med.	Mid	No	1.25	Upright bushy	Small to med.	Yes	Hardy
Ballerina	White, pink edge	Double	Med.	Late	No	0.5	Low dense	Med.	Yes	Low
Balsaminae Flora	Salmon	Full double	Med.	Late	No	0.4	Low spreading	Small	Yes	Hardy
Beatrix	Salmon orange	Double	Med.	Spot, early	No	0.8	Medium spreading	Med.	Yes	Average
Bertina	Salmon pink	Single	Large	Spot, mid	No	1	Medium bushy	Med.	Yes	Hardy
Betty Cuthbert	Pale pink	Hose-in-hose	Small	Mid	No	1	Dense bushy	Small	Yes	Hardy
Beverley Haerens	White	Double	Large	Spot, early	No	1	Spreading bushy	Med.	Yes	Average
Bonnie McKee	Deep mauve	Double	Large	Early/mid	No	1	Medium bushy	Med.	Yes	Average
Bride's Bouquet	White	Formal double	Small/med.	Mid	No	1	Upright bushy	Small	Yes	Average
California Peach	Peach pink	Double	Large	Spot, early	No	1	Spreading bushy	Med.	Yes	Average
Charlie	Purplish pink	Double	Med.	Long	No	0.8	Compact bushy	Med.	Yes	Average

52

	FLOWER FEATURES						PLANT FEATURES			
Variety	Colour	Type	Size	Timing	Sun	Height (m)	Growth Habit	Leaf Size	Tub Culture	Hardiness
Centenary Heritage	Salmon	Hose-in-hose	Med.	Mid/late	No	0.75	Spreading bushy	Med.	Yes	Average
Christmas Cheer	Carmine red	Single	Small	Early	No	0.75	Low compact	Small	Yes	Hardy
Christmas Pink	Pale mauve -pink	Double	Med.	Long	No	0.5	Low spreading	Med.	Yes	Low
Comtesse de Kerchove	Opal pink	Double	Med.	Early	No	0.8	Med. bushy	Med.	Yes	Average
Coral Wings	Salmon	Hose-in-hose	Med.	Spot, early	No	0.8	Spreading compact	Med.	Yes	Hardy
Dancer	Salmon pink	Semi-double	Med.	Spot, mid	No	1	Upright bushy	Med.	Yes	Hardy
Desert Rose	Salmon pink	Semi-double	Med.	Mid	No	0.8	Spreading	Med.	Yes	Average
Dogwood	Red,white edge	Single	Small	Late	Yes	1.5	Bushy	Med.	Yes	Hardy
Dogwood Red	Red	Single	Small	Late	Yes	1.5	Bushy	Med.	Yes	Hardy
Dogwood White	White	Single	Small	Late	Yes	1.5	Bushy	Med.	Yes	Hardy
Dr Arnold	Rose pink	Single	Large	Long	No	1.25	Spreading	Med.	Yes	Hardy
Dr Bergman	Orange red	Semi-double	Med.	Early	No	1	Upright bushy	Med.	Yes	Hardy
Duc de Rohan	Bright salmon	Single	Small	Mid/late	Yes	1.5	Upright bushy	Med.	Yes	Hardy
Elizabeth Lawrence	Violet	Single	Large	Early/ mid	Yes	1.75	Tall bushy	Large	No	Hardy
Elsa Karga	Spanish red	Double	Med.	Early/ mid	No	0.8	Med. bushy	Med.	Yes	Average
Emily Knights	Bright red	Single	Med.	Mid	No	1.25	Vigorous bushy	Med.	Yes	Hardy
Eri Schame	Pink and white	Semi-double	Med.	Long	No	0.8	Medium spreading	Med.	Yes	Average
Esmeralda	Pink	Single	Small	Mid	No	1.25	Upright bushy	Small	Yes	Hardy
Eureka	Pink and white	Double	Med.	Long	No	0.75	Low compact	Med.	Yes	Average
Exquisite	Lilac pink	Single	Large	Mid	Yes	2	Tall spreading	Large	No	Hardy
Fairy Bells	Pale pink flecked	Hose-in-hose	Med.	Long	No	1.5	Tall bushy	Med.	Yes	Hardy
Fairy Queen	Light pink	Semi-double hose-in-hose	Small	Mid	No	1.25	Upright bushy	Small	Yes	Hardy
Festival Queen	White	Semi-double	Large	Late	Yes	1.5	Upright bushy	Large	Yes	Hardy
Fielder's White	White	Single	Large	Mid	Yes	1.5	Upright bushy	Large	No	Hardy
Flamingo	Purple	Double	Med.	Long	Yes	1	Bushy	Med.	Yes	Hardy
Fred Colbert	Red	Semi-double hose-in-hose	Small	Mid	No	1	Compact bushy	Small	Yes	Hardy
Garden Party	Rose pink	Semi-double hose-in-hose	Long	Mid	No	1.25	Vigorous bushy	Large	Yes	Hardy

	FLOWER FEATURES						PLANT FEATURES			
Variety	Colour	Type	Size	Timing	Sun	Height (m)	Growth Habit	Leaf Size	Tub Culture	Hardiness
Geisha Girl	Cyclamen pink	Single	Large	Late	No	1	Spreading	Med.	Yes	Hardy
Glowing Embers	Orange red	Semi-double	Med.	Mid	No	1.25	Spreading	Med.	Yes	Hardy
Goyet	Bright red	Double	Large	Mid	Yes	1.25	Upright bushy	Large	Yes	Hardy
Gretel	White, cyclamen edge	Double	Med.	Mid/late	No	0.75	Low compact	Med.	Yes	Low
Guanda Pink	Apricot pink	Double	Large	Long	Yes	0.75	Bushy	Med.	Yes	Hardy
Guanda Red	Red	Double	Large	Long	Yes	0.75	Bushy	Med.	Yes	Hardy
Gumpo Petunia	Mauve	Single	Large	Late	No	0.5	Dense low	Small	Yes	Hardy
Gumpo Pink	Pink	Single	Large	Late	No	0.35	Dense low	Small	Yes	Hardy
Gumpo Salmon	Salmon	Single	Large	Late	No	0.35	Dense low	Small	Yes	Hardy
Gumpo Stripe	White with mauve	Single	Large	Late	No	0.5	Dense low	Small	Yes	Hardy
Gumpo White	White	Single	Large	Late	No	0.35	Dense low	Small	Yes	Hardy
Happy Days	Light purple	Double hose-in-hose	Med.	Long	No	1.25	Vigorous bushy	Med.	Yes	Hardy
Hatsu No Hana	White with salmon	Single	Large	Late	No	1	Dense spreading	Med.	Yes	Hardy
Helmut Vogel	Cerise	Double	Med.	Long	Yes	1	Bushy	Med.	Yes	Hardy
Higasa	Rose pink	Single	Large	Late	No	1	Spreading	Med.	Yes	Hardy
Inga	Pink, white edge	Double	Med.	Long	Yes	1	Bushy	Med.	Yes	Hardy
Issho No Haru	White and mauve	Single	Med.	Late	No	1	Spreading	Med.	Yes	Hardy
James Belton	Pale pink	Single	Med.	Mid	No	1.25	Bushy	Med.	Yes	Hardy
Janique	Orange red	Double	Large	Long	Yes	1.5	Bushy	Large	Yes	Hardy
Jean Alexandra	Pale pink	Single to semi-double	Med.	Early-mid	Yes	1.75	Tall bushy	Large	No	Hardy
Jennifer Ann	White	Double	Med.	Long	Yes	1.25	Medium bushy	Med.	Yes	Hardy
Jill Seymour	Pink, red stripe	Semi-double	Med.	M	No	1	Medium bushy	Med.	Yes	Hardy
Kalimna Pearl	Lavender pink	Double	Med.	Mid	Yes	2	Tall bushy	Large	No	Hardy
Kasane Kagaribi	Reddish-salmon	Single	Small	Mid	No	0.5	Low spreading	Small	Yes	Average
Kirin	Silvery rose-pink	Hose-in-hose	Small	Long	No	1.25	Medium bushy	Small	Yes	Hardy
Kosmos	Cerise	Double	Very large	Long	Yes	1	Bushy	Large	Yes	Hardy
Little Red Riding Hood	Orange red	Single	Small	Mid	No	0.75	Compact low	Small	Yes	Average

	FLOWER FEATURES						PLANT FEATURES			
Variety	Colour	Type	Size	Timing	Sun	Height (m)	Growth Habit	Leaf Size	Tub Culture	Hardiness
L.J. Bobbink	Lavender	Semi-double hose-in-hose	Med.	Late	Yes	1.5	Upright bushy	Med.	Yes	Hardy
Lucie	Rose pink	Double	Med.	Long	No	0.8	Compact bushy	Med.	Yes	Hardy
Lucille ëKí	Red, white edge	Single hose-in-hose	Med.	Long	Yes	1	Bushy spreading	Med.	Yes	Hardy
Madam Butterfly	Mauve	Double	Med.	Mid	Yes	1.5	Tall bushy	Large	No	Hardy
Madam Van Ackers	Cerise	Double	Med.	Long	No	0.8	Medium bushy	Med.	Yes	Average
Madame Auguste Haerens	Coral pink, white edge	Double	Large	Spot, early	No	1	Spreading bushy	Med.	Yes	Hardy
Madonna	White	Semi-double	Large	Mid	No	1	Medium bushy	Large	Yes	Hardy
Magnifica	Rosy violet	Single	Large	Mid	Yes	2	Tall spreading	Large	No	Hardy
Mardi Gras	Red, white edge	Single	Med.	Spot, mid	No	0.75	Compact bushy	Med.	Yes	Average
Martha Gardner	Spanish red	Double	Med.	Long	No	1	Compact bushy	Med.	Yes	Average
Maves	Bright red	Single	Med.	Mid	No	1.5	Tall	Med.	Yes	Average
Mission Bells	Red	Semi-double	Med.	Spot, mid	Yes	1	Medium bushy	Med.	Yes	Hardy
Mrs Gerda Kint	Pink, white edge	Single	Small to med.	Spot, mid	Yes	0.75	Low dense compact	Small	Yes	Hardy
Mrs Gerda Kint Alba	White	Single	Small to med.	Spot, mid	Yes	0.75	Low dense compact	Small	Yes	Hardy
My Fair Lady	Coral pink, white border	Double	Large	Spot, early	No	1	Spreading bushy	Med.	Yes	Average
Nancy Marie	White, red centre	Single	Small	Late	Yes	1.5	Bushy	Med.	Yes	Hardy
Neil Armstrong	Spanish red	Double	Large	Spot, mid	No	1.25	Upright bushy	Large	Yes	Hardy
Nuccio's Dewdrops	Blush pink, green throat	Single to semi-double	Small	Late	No	0.75	Compact bushy	Small-med.	Yes	Average
Only One Earth	Bright cerise	Semi-double	Med.	Early	No	1	Medium bushy	Med.	Yes	Average
Orange Chimes	Orange	Semi-double	Med.	Spot, early	No	1	Spreading	Med.	Yes	Average
Orange Delight	Bright orange	Single	Large	Spot, late	No	0.75	Spreading	Med.	Yes	Hardy
Orchidflora	Mauve pink	Semi-double	Large	Long	No	1.25	Upright bushy	Med.	Yes	Hardy
Orchidflora Alba	White	Semi-double	Large	Long	No	1.25	Upright bushy	Med.	Yes	Hardy
Orchidflora Pink	Pale pink, white edge	Semi-double	Large	Long	No	1.25	Upright bushy	Med.	Yes	Hardy
Orchidflora Salmon	Bright salmon pink	Semi-double	Large	Long	No	1.25	Upright bushy	Med.	Yes	Hardy
Osaraku	Lavender	Single	Small	Mid	No	1.25	Upright bushy	Small	Yes	Hardy
Osta	White, pink blotch	Single	Large	Mid	Yes	1.5	Bushy	Med.	Yes	Hardy

	FLOWER FEATURES					PLANT FEATURES				
Variety	Colour	Type	Size	Timing	Sun	Height (m)	Growth Habit	Leaf Size	Tub Culture	Hardiness
Osta Red	Red	Single	Large	Mid	Yes	1.5	Bushy	Med.	Yes	Hardy
Paloma	White	Double	Med.	Long	Yes	1	Bushy	Med.	Yes	Hardy
Paradise Charity	Soft pink	Double	Med.	Long	Yes	1	Bushy	Med.	Yes	Hardy
Paradise Coconut Ice	Two-tone pink	Double	Large	Mid	No	1	Bushy vigorous	Med.	Yes	Hardy
Paradise Elfin	Salmon	Hose-in-hose	Small	Mid	Yes	1	Bushy	Small	Yes	Hardy
Paradise Fiesta	White, pink stripes	Single to semi-double	Med.	Long	Yes	1	Vigorous bushy	Med.	Yes	Hardy
Paradise Honey	White, honey throat	Single	Large	Mid	Yes	1.5	Upright bushy	Med.	No	Hardy
Paradise Pixie	Rose pink	Hose-in-hose	Small	Mid	Yes	1	Bushy	Small	Yes	Hardy
Paradise Radiance	Deep rose pink	Hose-in-hose	Med.	Long	No	1	Bushy	Small	Yes	Hardy
Paradise Sensuous	Rose lavender	Double	Med.	Long	Yes	1.25	Upright bushy	Large	Yes	Hardy
Paradise Suzie	Blush pink, darker throat	Double	Med.	Long	Yes	1	Bushy	Med.	Yes	Hardy
Paradise Voodoo	Orange red	Hose-in-hose	Med.	Long	Yes	1	Bushy	Med.	Yes	Hardy
Paul Schame	Salmon red	Double	Med.	Long	No	0.8	Medium spreading	Med.	Yes	Average
Pauline Mardner	Bright pink	Semi-double	Med.	Long	No	1	Medium bushy	Med.	Yes	Hardy
Peach Blossom	Blush pink	Single	Small	Mid	No	1	Medium bushy	Small	Yes	Average
Petrick Alba	White	Double	Med.	Long	No	0.5	Low spreading	Med.	Yes	Low
Phil Sherringham	White to lavender	Double	Med.	Mid	No	1.25	Bushy	Med.	Yes	Hardy
Phoenicea	Violet rose	Single	Large	Mid	Yes	1.75	Tall vigorous	Med.	No	Hardy
Phryne	Creamy white	Double	Med.	Mid	No	1	Medium bushy	Small	Yes	Average
Pink Dream	Soft pink	Single	Large	Long	No	1.25	Spreading	Med.	Yes	Hardy
Pink Lace	Pink, white edge	Single	Small	Mid/late	Yes	1.5	Upright bushy	Med.	Yes	Hardy
Pink Ruffles	Pink and white	Double	Med.	Long	No	0.8	Bushy	Med. twisted	Yes	Average
Pink Tiger	Red spotted, lavender pink	Single	Med.	Late	No	1.5	Tall bushy	Med.	Yes	Hardy
Pride of Dorking	Carmine red	Single	Med.	Late	Yes	2	Tall bushy	Med.	No	Hardy
Princess Maude	Cerise	Single	Med.	Mid	Yes	1.25	Medium bushy	Small to med.	Yes	Hardy
Purple Glitters	Bright purple	Single	Small to med.	Mid	No	1	Dense bushy	Small to med.	Yes	Average
Red Line	White, flecked pink	Double	Med.	Long	No	0.8	Medium spreading	Med.	Yes	Average

	FLOWER FEATURES						PLANT FEATURES			
Variety	Colour	Type	Size	Timing	Sun	Height (m)	Growth Habit	Leaf Size	Tub Culture	Hardiness
Red Poppy	Dark red	Single to semi-double	Med.	Spot, early	Yes	1.25	Medium bushy	Med.	Yes	Hardy
Red Ruffles	Salmon rose	Double	Med.	Long	No	0.8	Bushy	Med. twisted	Yes	Average
Redwing	Bright red	Single hose-in-hose	Med.	Long	Yes	1	Bushy spreading	Med.	Yes	Hardy
Ripples	Rose red	Double	Med.	Long	No	0.75	Low compact	Small	Yes	Average
Rosa Belton	White, mauve edge	Single	Med.	Mid	No	1.25	Bushy	Med.	Yes	Hardy
Rosa Lee	Bright cerise	Hose-in-hose	Small	Spot, mid	No	1	Dense bushy	Small	Yes	Hardy
Rosalie	Mauve pink	Semi-double	Med.	Mid	No	1	Bushy	Med.	Yes	Average
Rose King	Deep rose pink	Semi-double	Med.	Long	No	1	Bushy	Med.	Yes	Hardy
Rose Magnifica	Rose pink	Single	Large	Mid	Yes	2	Tall spreading	Large	No	Hardy
Rose Queen	Bright pink	Semi-double	Med.	Long	No	1	Bushy	Med.	Yes	Hardy
Rosina	Soft pink	Double	Med.	Mid	No	1	Upright bushy	Med.	Yes	Average
Ruth Kirk	Salmon pink	Single	Med./ large	Early	No	1	Medium bushy	Med.	Yes	Average
Saidee Kirk	Shell pink	Double	Med.	Mid	No	1.25	Vigorous bushy	Med.	Yes	Hardy
Scarlet Gem	Orange scarlet	Hose-in hose	Small/ med.	Mid	No	0.75	Medium bushy	Small	Yes	Average
Schryderii	White, lilac throat	Single	Med./ large	Spot, mid	Yes	1.5	Tall bushy	Hairy large	No	Hardy
Schryderii Mauve	Pale mauve	Single	Med./ large	Spot, mid	Yes	1.5	Tall bushy	Hairy large	No	Hardy
Searchlight	White	Double	Med.	Long	No	0.5	Low bushy	Med.	Yes	Low
Seikai	White	Semi-double hose-in-hose	Small	Mid	No	1	Compact bushy	Small	Yes	Average
September Bells	Bright salmon	Single	Small/ med.	Late	No	1	Upright bushy	Small/ med.	Yes	Average
Seraphim	Pale pink, spotted throat	Hose-in-hose	Small/ med.	Mid	No	1	Medium bushy	Small/ med.	Yes	Hardy
Shin-Kyo	Salmon pink, darker edges	Single	Med.	Late	No	1	Upright bushy	Med.	Yes	Hardy
Silver Anniversary	Pale pink	Single to semi-double hose-in-hose	Med.	Mid	No	1	Medium bushy	Med.	Yes	Hardy
Snow Prince	White	Semi-double	Med.	Long	No	1	Bushy	Med.	Yes	Hardy
Snowflake	White	Single hose-in-hose	Small	Mid	No	1	Compact bushy	Small	Yes	Average
Southern Aurora	Apricot salmon	Double	Med.	Early	No	0.75	Medium bushy	Med.	Yes	Average
Special Occasion	Candy pink	Single	Med.	Late	No	1	Medium bushy	Med.	Yes	Average
Splendens	Salmon pink	Single	Med.	Mid	Yes	2	Bushy upright	Med.	No	Hardy

	FLOWER FEATURES						PLANT FEATURES			
Variety	Colour	Type	Size	Timing	Sun	Height (m)	Growth Habit	Leaf Size	Tub Culture	Hardiness
Starlight	Salmon pink	Double	Med.	Late	No	0.75	Bushy	Med.	Yes	Average
Stella Maris	Pinkish white	Single	Med.	Late	Yes	1	Bushy	Med.	Yes	Hardy
Sui-Yohi	Flesh pink, salmon edges	Incomplete hose-in-hose	Small	Mid	No	1	Dense bushy	Small	Yes	Hardy
Sweet Nellie	Cerise	Semi-double hose-in-hose	Small/ med.	Mid	No	0.75	Spreading	Med.	Yes	Hardy
Teena Maree	Salmon pink	Semi-double hose-in-hose	Med.	Spot, mid	No	1.25	Vigorous bushy	Med.	Yes	Hardy
Temperance	Mauve	Semi-double	Med.	Mid	No	1.25	Tall bushy	Med.	Yes	Average
Terra Nova	Baby pink	Double	Med.	Long	Yes	1	Bushy	Med.	Yes	Hardy
The Teacher	Pink, edged with dark pink	Semi-double	Med.	Mid	No	1	Medium bushy	Med.	Yes	Hardy
Thelma Bray	Mauve, white throat	Semi-double	Small/ med/	Mid	No	1	Bushy	Med.	Yes	Average
Trisha Tilley	White	Semi-double hose-in-hose	Small	Mid	No	0.75	Low spreading	Small	Yes	Hardy
Versicolour	Cream, splashed salmon	Double	Med.	Long	No	0.8	Medium spreading	Med.	Yes	Average
Violacea	Deep violet	Double	Med.	Spot, early	No	0.75	Bushy spreading	Small/ med.	Yes	Average
Violetta	Soft violet	Semi-double hose-in-hose	Small	Mid	No	0.75	Compact	Small	Yes	Hardy
Waka Kayede	Cerise crimson	Single	Small/ med.	Mid	Yes	1.2	Bushy upright	Small	Yes	Hardy
Ward's Ruby	Blood red	Single	Small	Late	No	1	Bushy	Small	Yes	Hardy
White Bouquet	White, green throat	Semi-double	Med./ large	Spot, early	Yes	1	Bushy spreading	Med.	Yes	Hardy
White Gish	White	Semi-double hose-in-hose	Med.	Spot, mid	No	1	Bushy	Med.	Yes	Average
White Lace	White	Single	Small	Mid to late	Yes	1.5	Upright bushy	Med.	Yes	Hardy
White Prince	White, red throat	Semi-double	Med.	Long	No	1	Bushy	Med.	Yes	Hardy
White Schame	White	Semi-double	Med.	Long	No	0.8	Medium spreading	Med.	Yes	Average

Index

(numbers in *italics* indicate page number of colour illustration)